Hotel convention English

호텔컨벤션영어

길우경 · 한진영

지식인

Authors

길우경

가톨릭관동대학교 호텔경영학과 교수

고등학교 시절부터 미국생활을 했고, 뉴욕주립대학에서 영어교육학 전공으로 석사학위를 받았고, 프랑스 파리3대학에서 불어불문학 전공으로 박사학위를 받았다. 1988년부터 가톨릭관동대학교에서 프랑스어와 영어를 가르치고 있다.

저서에는 『엣지 있는 영어회화 For Your Tour』, 『Hotel English(호텔영어)』, 『Hotel·Tourism English(호텔·관광영어)』, 『프랑스 문화여행』 등이 있다.

한진영

가톨릭관동대학교 호텔경영학과 교수

경희대학교에서 국제회의이벤트학 전공으로 석사학위를 받았고, 세종대학교에서 호텔관광경영학 전공으로 박사학위를 받았으며, 2009년부터 가톨릭관동대학교에서 컨벤션 과목들을 강의하고 있다.

저서에는 『컨벤션경영론』, 『컨벤션기획실무론』, 『호텔경영학개론』, 『호텔이벤트경영론』 등이 있다.

Hotel Convention English

호텔컨벤션영어

2018년 1월 20일 초판 1쇄 인쇄
2018년 1월 25일 초판 1쇄 발행

지은이 | 길우경 · 한진영
펴낸이 | 김종욱
펴낸곳 | 지식인
등 록 | 제301-2013-134호
주 소 | 서울시 도봉구 도봉로 180길 20 투웨니퍼스트 102동 602호
전 화 | 02)2266-8606 (대)
팩 스 | 02)2266-8607
E-mail | jisikin2013@naver.com
홈페이지 | www.jisikinbook.co.kr

ISBN 979-11-88105-16-8 (93740)

값 17,000원

Hotel Convention English

호텔컨벤션영어

P R E F A C E

언어를 배우기 위한 가장 필수적인 요소는 흥미일 것이다. 2000년 봄, 안식년으로 뉴욕주립대학(SUNY at Albany)에 머물 때 인상 깊게 들었던 인터뷰 내용이 기억난다. UCLA의 한 언어학 교수였는데, "모국어가 아닌 다른 언어를 배우고 다른 문화를 배운다는 것은 마치 섹스와도 같다. 그것은 본질적으로 즐거움을 주는 일이다."(Learning about another language and about another culture, is like sex. It is intrinsically pleasurable.)라고 확신했다.
외국어를 배우는 과정이 무조건 즐겁기만 하겠는가. 필자는 외국어 학습에 점차 흥미를 잃어 중도에 포기하는 학생들을 수없이 지켜봐 왔다. 낯선 언어를 반복 학습하는데 따르는 지루함을 견디어내는 인내와 끈기가 있어야 즐거움을 기대할 수 있을 것이다.

이 책은 대학에서 호텔컨벤션영어를 이수하는 학생들과 호텔관련 영어가 필요한 일반인들이 흥미를 느낄 수 있도록 다양한 코너를 준비한 영어학습서이다. 전반부는 호텔업무와 관련된 제반상황을 8개 Unit으로 나누어 각 상황에서 발생할 수 있는 여러 가지 사례를 대화 형식으로 수록했고, 해외 여러 나라의 문화와 관광명소를 돌아보는 코너를 각 장마다 삽입하여 세계에 대한 호기심을 자극하고자 했다. 후반부는 컨벤션영어에 중점을 두고 프레젠테이션을 할 때나 컨벤션기획시에 필요한 다양한 표현과 영문편지 사례를 소개했고, 특히 흥미는 기본적으로 새로움에서 온다는 생각으로 오래된 자료보다는 최신자료를 수록하려고 애썼다. 예를 들어, 국제회의 개회사와 폐회사의 샘플자료는 가장 최근의 것으로, 동시통역을 맡고 있는 지인의 도움을 받았다.
따라서 이 책은 전반부에서는 호텔영어를 중심으로, 후반부에는 컨벤션영어를 중심으로 구성했고, 전반부의 각 Unit은 다섯 부분으로 구성되어 있다. 첫 번째 부분은 상황별 회화[Dialogue], 두 번째는 핵심단어들을 학습하는 코너인 어휘퀴즈[Vocabulary], 세 번째는 해외명소를 투어하고 각 나라의 문화를 엿볼 수 있는 글로벌투어[Global Countries & Culture], 네 번째는 토익문제풀이를 통해 영어문법을 정리한 [TOEIC Tips]. 그리고 마지막으로는 세계 유명호텔 홈페이지에 들어가 호텔홍보 동영상을 비롯한 여러 퀴즈를 풀어보는 [Exercise]이다.

컨벤션영어 중심의 후반부에서는, 각 Unit을 여섯 부분으로 나누었다. 첫 번째 코너에서는 컨퍼런스를 유치하기 위해 시설을 홍보하는 발표문을 비롯하여 국제회의에서 행해지는 개회사와 폐회사에 이르기까지 여러 장르의 연설문을 학습하고, 뒤이어 컨벤션 관련 영문편지의 작성요령을 살펴보고[Writing Tips], 세 번째와 네 번째는 전반부와 똑같이 어휘퀴즈[Vocabulary]와 글로벌투어[Global Countries & Culture], 다섯 번째는 컨벤션기획사 영어시험문제를 풀어보는 코너로, 그리고 마지막으로는 컨퍼런스 참가자들에게 보내는 안내장 작성에서부터 국제회의 연사들에게 보내는 감사장에 이르기까지 다양한 홍보편지와 초대장을 영어로 직접 작성해보는 [Exercise]이다.

이 책의 학습자들이 성실한 인내로 전문가의 길을 향해 매진하기를 희망한다. 꾸준한 영어학습을 통해 국제화시대에 걸맞는 영어로의 의사소통 능력을 갖춘 컨벤션기획사가 되기를, 세계 어디에 내놓아도 손색이 없는 자랑스러운 호텔리어가 되기를 기대한다.

저자 길우경 & 한진영

CONTENTS

UNIT 1 **Taking a Reservation (객실 예약받기)** 007
Dialogue / Vocabulary
Global Countries and Culture : 독일의 라인강
TOEIC Tips
Exercise : 뉴욕의 Waldorf Astoria호텔

UNIT 2 **Checking-in (체크인하기)** 019
Dialogue / Vocabulary
Global Countries and Culture : 독일 베를린
TOEIC Tips
Exercise : 미국 나파벨리의 바르데소노호텔

UNIT 3 **Taking Phone Calls and Messages (전화와 메시지 받기)** 033
Dialogue / Vocabulary
Global Countries and Culture : 스페인 세빌리아
TOEIC Tips
Exercise : 서울의 비스타 워커힐호텔

UNIT 4 **Hotel Service (호텔서비스)** 045
Dialogue / Vocabulary
Global Countries and Culture : 스페인 마드리드
TOEIC Tips
Exercise : 파리 리츠호텔

UNIT 5 **Serving in the Bar (바에서 서빙하기)** 057
Dialogue / Vocabulary
Global Countries and Culture : 영국
TOEIC Tips
Exercise : 런던의 사보이호텔

UNIT 6 **Taking Orders in the Restaurant (식당에서 주문받기)** 069
Dialogue / Vocabulary
Global Countries and Culture : 영국
TOEIC Tips
Exercise : 그리스 산토리니의 Dreams Luxury Suites호텔

UNIT 7 **Dealing with Requests (고객의 요구 해결하기)** 083
Dialogue / Vocabulary
Global Countries and Culture : 벨기에
TOEIC Tips
Exercise : 뉴욕의 플라자호텔

C O N T E N T S

UNIT 8 **Checking-out (체크아웃하기)** 095
Dialogue / Vocabulary
Global Countries and Culture : 네덜란드
TOEIC Tips
Exercise : Necker Island

UNIT 9 **For Convention(I) (프레젠테이션)** 107
Presentation / Writing Tips / Vocabulary
Global Countries and Culture : 이탈리아의 로마
컨벤션기획사 영어시험문제
Exercise : 홍보용 편지 작성

UNIT 10 **For Convention(II) (프레젠테이션)** 125
Presentation / Writing Tips / Vocabulary
Global Countries and Culture : 이탈리아의 베니스
컨벤션기획사 영어시험문제
Exercise : 회의참가자 등록양식 작성

UNIT 11 **For Convention(III) (프레젠테이션 – 질의 응답)** 143
Questions & Answers / Writing Tips / Vocabulary
Global Countries and Culture : 스칸디나비아 헬싱키
컨벤션기획사 영어시험문제
Exercise : 안내장 작성

UNIT 12 **For Convention(IV) (국제회의)** 159
개회사 / Writing Tips / Vocabulary
Global Countries and Culture : 스칸디나비아 스톡홀름
컨벤션기획사 영어시험문제
Exercise : 노벨상 시상식 초청장 작성

UNIT 13 **For Convention(V) (국제회의)** 177
폐회사 / Writing Tips / Vocabulary
Global Countries and Culture : 프랑스 파리
컨벤션기획사 영어시험문제
Exercise : 만찬초대장 작성

UNIT 14 **For Convention(VI) (국제회의)** 195
축사 / Writing Tips / Vocabulary
Global Countries and Culture : 프랑스 노르망디
컨벤션기획사 영어시험문제
Exercise : 감사편지 작성

UNIT 1

Taking a Reservation

Hotel
convention
English

호텔컨벤션영어

Dialogue

1.

Receptionist: Good morning, Grand Hotel. How can I help you?

Guest: Good morning. I'd like to make a reservation for the third weekend in April. The 24th and the 25th. Do you have a double room available?

Receptionist: Yes, we do.

Guest: Good. How much is it?

Receptionist: It's three hundred dollars per night including breakfast.

Guest: That's fine.

Receptionist: May I have your name?

Guest: Charles Robinson.

Receptionist: Could you spell your last name for me, please?

Guest: Sure. R-O-B-I-N-S-O-N

Receptionist: And is there a phone number where you can be contacted?

Guest: Yes, my cell phone number is 010-5552-6386.

Receptionist: All right, Mr. Robinson. Your reservation has been made for the twenty-fourth of April for a room with a double bed. Check-in is at 2 o'clock.

Guest: Great, thank you.

Receptionist: My pleasure. We'll see you in April, Mr. Robinson. Have a nice day.

Notes

available a.

① 이용할 수 있는, 쓸모있는

② 손에 넣을 수 있는, 이용 가능한

③ (일 따위에) 전심할 수 있는, 손이 비어 있는, 여가가 있는

ex) a train available for second-class passengers 이등승객용 열차

tickets available on the day of issue 발행 당일만 유효한 표

Are you available? 시간 좀 있니? 우리 만날 수 있을까?

He is not available for the job. 그는(달리 일이 있어) 이일에는 쓸 수 없다.

2.

Receptionist: The Grand Lakewood Hotel. What can I do for you?

Guest: Do you have a suite room available on July 7th?

Receptionist: Yes sir, we have several rooms available for that date. How many people are there in your party?

Guest: There will be two of us.

Receptionist: Great. And would you prefer to have a suite room with a view of the ocean?

Guest: If that type of room is available, I would love to have an ocean view. What's the rate for the room?

Receptionist: Your room is five hundred and ninety dollars per night. Now may I have your name please?

Guest: My name is Minsoo Kim.

Receptionist: How can we contact you, sir?

Guest: You can call me at 010-5341-2100. It's my cell number.

Receptionist: How would you like to pay your account, sir?

Guest: Let me pay by traveller's check.

Receptionist: Okay. You're confirmed from July 7th to 8th in a suit room. If

	there's anything else I can help you with, just let me know, sir.
Guest:	Thank you. Bye.

Notes

suite n.

① (가구 따위의) 한 벌, [음악] 모음곡

② 붙은 방(호텔 따위에서 침실 외에 거실이나 응접실에 붙어있는 것)

confirm vt.

① 확실히 하다, 확증하다

② 확인하다, 유효함을 확인하다

ex) This report confirms my suspicions. 이 보고로 내 의심이 확인되었다.
Did you confirm our flight reservation? 우리 비행기예약을 확인했니?

3.

Guest:	I'd like to reserve a room for this weekend, please.
Receptionist:	I'm sorry, ma'am. we're fully booked for that weekend.
Guest:	Then, how about this Thursday for two nights for two people?
Receptionist:	Let me check. We have a double room available.
Guest:	I'll take it.
Receptionist:	Ok, that will be $210 including breakfast. And you name, ma'am?
Guest:	Lisa Taylor.
Receptionist:	All right, Mrs. Taylor. I'm looking forward to seeing you on Thursday evening. Goodbye!

Notes

look forward to a thing (doing)

~을 기대하다, ~을 즐거움으로 기다리다

Vocabulary

Write the word that best completes each sentence.

accommodation, booked, transportation, confirm, concierge

1. To verify is to ________________.

2. ________________ is a means of traveling from one place to another.

3. The ________________ greets arriving guests.

4. ________________ is the place where one sleeps when traveling.

5. We don't have any vacancies. We are completely ________________.

Global Countries and Culture

Germany
Romantic Rhine and Rothenburg

독일을 상징하는 대표적인 것이 라인강이며, 그 중 마인츠와 쾰른 사이의 라인강이 가장 낭만적이다. 배를 타고 로렐라이 언덕을 지나서 로맨틱한 라인강 지역을 여행한다. 주변의 환상적인 고성들은 탄성을 자아낸다.

Today the Rhine castles are enjoyed as restaurants, hotels, hostels, and museums. And travelers cruise the river just to castle-watch. Tour boats come and go about hourly. Various lines each have their own docks and advertise their own schedules. Buying tickets from a kiosk before boarding, tourists can put together their own hop-on and hop-off tours of this most romantic stretch of the Rhine.

Along with transporting camera-toting tourists, the Rhine moves a steady flow of cargo to the world's biggest port — Rotterdam — which waits at the mouth of the river. Barge workers are almost a subculture. Many own their own ships. The captain and his family live in the stern — car parked on the rooftop. The crew lives in the bow. Logically, imports — like oil — go upstream, and exports — like German manufactured goods — go downstream.

The powerful Rhine has long been treacherous to navigate. Boats generally pass on the right. Since downstream ships can't stop or maneuver as freely, upstream boats are expected to do the tricky do-si-do work. Large triangular signals, posted before troublesome blind bends in the river, warn of oncoming ships.

Each triangle covers a segment of the bend — the lowest triangle being nearest. They warn of approaching ships. If the bottom side of a triangle is lit, that sector is empty. But if the left side is lit, there's an oncoming ship in that sector.

The most dangerous bend in the river swings around a rocky bluff called the Loreley. Because of reefs just upstream, many ships never made it safely past the Loreley, and the rocky cliff remains steeped in myth.

Sailors blamed their misfortune on a Fräulein so wunderbar her long blonde hair almost covered her body. This legendary siren flirted and sang her distracting songs from this rock.

[출처] https://www.ricksteves.com

TOEIC Tips

1. According to the sales manager, discount vouchers are available __________ to regular customers of our hotel restaurants.

(A) exclusive (B) exclusively

(C) inclusive (D) inclusively

[해석] 영업부장에 의하면, 할인권은 우리 호텔 레스토랑의 단골고객들에게만 이용이 가능하다.
[해설] available(이용할 수 있는)은 2형식 문의 보어인 형용사로 쓰였으므로, 그것을 후위 수식하는 부사 (B) exclusively (독점적으로, 다른 곳에서는 입수할 수 없도록)가 와야 한다. (A) exclusive(독점적인)와 (C) inclusive(포함한, 포괄적인)는 형용사라서 쓸 수 없고, (D) inclusively(포함하여)는 문맥상 의미가 맞지 않는다. 정답 I B

2. The five-star hotel, such as Grand Intercontinental Seoul Parnasse, is __________. considered to be one of the hotels in this country favored by students who are majoring in Hotel Management.

(A) general (B) generally

(C) individual (D) individually

[해석] 그랜드 인터콘티넨탈 서울 파르나스와 같은 5성급 호텔은 호텔경영학을 전공하는 학생들이 선호하는 우리나라 특급호텔 중 하나다.
[해설] 동사 consider(고려하다, …으로 여기다)를 수식하는 부사가 와야 한다. 그러므로 여기서는 부사 generally(일반적으로, 대개는)와 individually(개인적으로, 독자적 방법으로) 둘 중 하나를 골라야 한다. generally와 individually는 상반되는 개념이기 때문에 문맥상 (B) generally가 맞는 표현이다. (A) general와 (C) individual은 형용사이므로 수동태 문형 be+p.p.에서 be동사와 p.p.의 사이에 놓일 수 없고, (D) individually은 의미가 다른 부사이므로 문맥상 사용될 수 없다. 정답 I B

3. As the managing director Mr. Hong was faced with the reduction in hotel staff because of the serious economic recession, he __________ to Seong-yeon, a staff member of the hotel, that he apply for the job advertised in the Job Fair last weekend.

(A) suggestion (B) suggesting

(C) suggested (D) suggest

[해석] 심한 경기불황으로 호텔 직원을 감축해야 하는 홍 사장은 호텔 직원인 승연에게 지난주 취업박람회에서 광고된 그 일자리에 지원해보라고 제안했다.

[해설] 주절의 문맥상 과거형 술어동사가 필요한 문제다. 문장의 맨 끝에 단순과거를 나타내는 last가 쓰였기 때문에, 정답은 suggested(제안했다)이다. (A) suggestion은 명사이므로 불가능하고, (B) suggesting은 동명사이므로 suggest 다음에 목적어가 와야 한다. (D) suggest는 현재시제이므로 suggest에 s가 붙어야 한다. 정답 I C

4. The responsibilities of the reception desk of our hotel are calculating various bills and writing ___________.

(A) reporters (B) reportable

(C) reports (D) reportage

[해석] 우리 호텔의 접수계가 담당하고 있는 업무는 각종 계산서를 계산하고 보고서를 작성하는 일이다.

[해설] 이 문장은 2형식 문형의 주어 responsibilities의 보어를 찾는 문제이다. 즉 calculating A and writing B에서 등위접속사 and를 사이에 두고 A와 대등한 역할을 하는 명사를 B에 놓으면 된다. (A) reporter(보고자, 통신원)는 사람이므로 writing의 목적어가 될 수 없고, (D) reportage(보도활동, 취재활동)는 추상명사로서 writing과 연결되면 '보도활동을 쓰다'라는 어색한 표현이 되며, (B) reportable(보도할 가치가 있는)는 형용사이기 때문에 목적어 역할을 할 수 없다. 정답 I C

5. The receptionist at the Four Seasons Hotel Bangkok quickly and courteously ___________ the foreign trade mission to the italian restaurant of the hotel.

(A) guiding (B) guided

(C) guider (D) guide

[해석] 방콕에 있는 포 시즌스 호텔의 접수계원은 외국에서 온 무역사절단을 그 호텔의 이탈리아 레스토랑으로 신속하고 정중하게 안내했다.

[해설] '주어+guide A to B : 주어가 A를 B로 안내하다'의 구문으로 된 문장에서 필요한 것은 주어 receptionist의 동작을 서술하는 술어동사이다. (A) guiding은 분사로서 앞에 be동사가 오면 현재진행형 구문이 된다. (D) guide는 현재시제이므로 주어가 3인칭 단수일 때는 s를 붙여야 하고, (C) guider(안내인)는 사람이므로 술어동사의 자리에 올 수 없다. 정답 I B

6. **The ___________ is considering hiring new members of staff because of the completion of its large scale renovation of the hotel.**

(A) manage　　(B) management

(C) managing　　(D) manageable

[해석] 호텔의 대규모 수리가 끝남에 따라 경영진은 신규직원 채용을 고려하고 있다.

[해설] 정관사 the 뒤에는 명사가 와야 한다. the는 뒤에 오는 명사를 한정시키는 한정사(determiner)의 역할을 하기 때문이다. (B) management(경영, 관리, 경영진)은 the를 붙이면 '경영(관리)진'의 의미가 된다. (A) manage(…를 경영하다)는 동사, (D) manageable(처리할 수 있는, 다루기 쉬운)은 형용사이다. (C) managing은 동명사로서 뒤에 목적어가 와야 한다. 정답 I B

Exercise

Waldorf Astoria호텔은 미국 뉴욕에 위치하고 있는 특급호텔입니다. 얼마 전 힐튼호텔에 합류하여 글로벌호텔로 거듭나게 되었지요. 두 개의 따로 존재하던 Waldorf호텔과 Astoria호텔을 하나로 통합하면서 한동안은 그 이름이 Waldorf-Astoria로 단어 사이에 (—)부호를 넣어서 사용했지요. 그래서 뉴욕의 연인들이 만남의 장소로 "Meet me at the Hyphen!"이라고 말하면 그 호텔이라는 것을 모두 알아들었다고 합니다.
이 호텔의 탄생 일화에 대해 알아볼까요?

[출처] www.businesstravel.fr(Hilton vend le Waldorf Astoria New York)

UNIT 2

Checking-in

Hotel
convention
English

호텔컨벤션영어

Dialogue

1.

Receptionist:	Good afternoon, sir. Can I help you?
Guest:	I'd like to check in, please. It's under the name of Wylie.
Receptionist:	Yes, Mr. Wylie, let me check. We've reserved a double room for you with a view of the ocean for two nights. Is that correct?
Guest:	Yes, it is.
Receptionist:	You are in room 408. Would you please fill in this registration card?
Guest:	Yes, of course. Do I fill in my home address?
Receptionist:	Yes, please. And could I have your passport? Thank you. Here's your key card for the room 408. How would you like to pay for the room?
Guest:	Do you take American Express?
Receptionist:	Certainly, sir.
Guest:	Do I pay now or when I check out?
Receptionist:	In advance, please.
Guest:	Here we go.
Receptionist:	Thank you. Enjoy your stay.

Notes

registration n.

기입, 등기, 등록, 기명, (우편물의) 등기

ex) registration card 숙박부

fill in

(구멍, 틈을) 메우다, (서류, 빈 곳에) 써 넣다, (필요사항을) 적어 넣다

ex) Fill in this application form. 신청서에 필요사항을 채워 넣다.

2.

Guest:	Hi, my name is Robert Hong and I made a reservation.
Receptionist:	Let me check, sir. Ok, I just need you to fill in this form please. Do you want breakfast?
Guest:	Yes, please.
Receptionist:	Breakfast is from 7 to 10 each morning in the dining room. Here is your key. Your room number is 345, on the third floor. How will you be paying for your account?
Guest:	I'll be paying with Mastercard.
Receptionist:	Oh, I'm, very sorry, sir. The hotel does not accept Mastercard. Do you have other cards?
Guest:	My goodness! I forgot to ask when I made the reservation. I use only Mastercard.
Receptionist:	There's a bank just opposite the hotel that might be able to help you.
Guest:	I see. Thanks anyway.

Notes

account n.

① 계산, 셈, 계산서, 청구서

② 계정, 예금계좌

ex) open an account with ~와 거래를 시작하다, (은행)에 계좌를 트다

pay an account 셈을 끝내다

put ~ to a person's account ~을 아무의 셈에 달다

3.

Receptionist: Welcome to the Breeze Hotel. How may I help you, sir?

James: Yes, my name is James Bond. I have a reservation here.

Receptionist: Wait a moment, sir. I'm sorry, Mr. Bond, but there is no record of your booking.

James: There must be a mistake. Anyway I need a twin room for tonight. My wife and I had a long flight and we're exhausted now.

Receptionist: I'm afraid we are fully booked until the end of this month. This is the peak season.

James: You are saying there is no room in your hotel? Honestly speaking, I made my reservation a month ago.

Receptionist: Who did you talk to, sir?

James: Well, it was Mona, I think.

Receptionist: Unfortunately she's on medical leave today.

James: Great! Are you sure there is no room left?

Receptionist: Let me check again, sir. Well, as a matter of fact, we do have a suite available, it's $700 per night.

James: You gotta be kidding. I can't afford it. I just want to talk to your manager now.

Receptionist: I'll get him right away. Please wait, Mr Bond.

Notes

exhausted a.

다 써버린 소모된, 고갈된, 지쳐 빠진 [SYN.] ⇨ tired

peak n.

① (뾰족한) 끝, 첨단

② 산꼭대기, 봉우리

③ 절정, 최고점

ex) Traffic reaches its peak about 7 o'clock.

medical leave

생리휴가, 보건휴가

afford vt.

~의 여유가 있다, ~을 지불할 돈이 있다

ex) I can't afford the expense. 그 비용을 감당할 수 없다.

Vocabulary

Write the word that best completes each sentence.

satisfaction, vending machine, availability, valet, out

1. _______________ is whether something is easily accessible or not.

2. We do not have a _______________ service. You'll have to park your car yourself.

3. The room has a pull _______________ couch, so it will sleep an extra person.

4. _______________ is 'gratification', 'pleasure' or 'contentment'.

5. If you need a midnight snack there's a _______________ full of potato chips on your floor.

Global Countries and Culture

Germany
Berlin

1990년 통일 이후, 독일연방공화국의 수도가 된 베를린에는 20세기의 복잡한 역사를 담고 있는 기념물이 많다. 'Forgive but never forget'의 문구가 쓰여 있는 이 곳 홀로코스트 기념관은 매년 독일인 초등학교 학생들을 포함한 세계의 많은 방문객들이 찾고 있다.

Berlin is dotted with memorials and reminders of its troubled 20th-century history.

For a man with such megalomaniac ambitions, it's striking how little survives of the world Hitler created. The former headquarters of the Nazi air force, or Luftwaffe, now houses the German Finance Ministry. It's the only major Hitler-era building that — somehow — survived the war's bombs. Notice how the Fascist architecture is monumental, making the average person feel small and powerless.

Just down the street, an exhibition called the "Topography of Terror"is built upon the bombed out remains of the notorious SS and Gestapo buildings. This spot, once the most feared address in Berlin, documents the methods and evils of the Nazi regime.

Nearby is a sight with nothing to see: a parking lot — vacant…yet thought-provoking. It's the site of Hitler's vast underground bunker. In early 1945, as

Allied armies advanced on Berlin and Nazi Germany lay in ruins, Hitler and his inner circle retreated here.

It was right here, deep in his underground bunker, that Hitler committed suicide…on April 30, 1945. A week later, the war in Europe was over.

In their attempt to exterminate the Jewish race, the Nazis killed six million Jews. Berlin's Holocaust memorial is a touching and evocative field of gravestone-like pillars. Called the "Memorial to the Murdered Jews of Europe," it was the first formal, German government-sponsored Holocaust memorial.

When Germany called this a memorial to the "murdered" Jews it was a big step. They admitted to a crime. They did it. The design of this memorial has no explicit meaning. It's hoped that each visitor will find their own.

There's no central gathering point; it's for individuals, like death. Once you enter the memorial, people seem to appear and then disappear. Is it a labyrinth? A symbolic cemetery? Intentionally disorienting? It's entirely up to you to derive the meaning, while pondering this horrible chapter in human history.

[출처] https://www.ricksteves.com

TOEIC Tips

1. Rosa L. Parks was an African-American civil ________ activist, whom the U.S. Congress called "the mother of the freedom movement".

(A) right (B) rights

(C) rightfulness (D) righter

[해석] 로사 엘 팍스는 미 의회가 "자유운동의 어머니"라고 불렀던 아프리카계 미국인 민권 운동가였다. (*팍스 여사는 앨라배마 주 몽고메리에서 일어났던 "몽고메리 버스 보이콧" 사건의 중심인물이었고, 마틴 루터 킹 목사와 더불어 1950년대 미국 민권운동을 이끈 미국인들의 가장 존경받는 인물 중 한 사람이었다.)

[해설] 빈 칸에 들어갈 명사는 'rights(공민권)'를 의미하는 말이다. 인권은 human rights, 민권은 civil rights라고 한다. (A) right는 '권리'를 뜻하며, 복수형 rights와 구분된다. (C)는 '정통성', (D)는 '정의를 행하는 사람'을 의미한다.

정답 I B

2. Strictly speaking, new staff members need. ________ from their senior members to solve the formidable tasks.

(A) advice (B) advise

(C) advices (D) adviser

[해석] 엄밀히 말해서, 신입사원들은 힘든 과제들을 해결하기 위해서 그들의 선임자들로부터 조언을 들을 필요가 있다.

[해설] 술어동사 need의 목적어가 되는 가산·불가산명사에 관한 문제이다. 조언을 나타내는 advice는 추상명사이므로 불가산명사이다. 그러므로 단수명사 advice가 와야 한다. (B)는 동사 '조언하다'이며, (D)는 조언을 하는 사람이다.

정답 I A

3. The article about "Trade Dispute Threatens European Wine ________ to China" appeared in Wine Spectator, July 24, 2013.

(A) sale (B) sales

(C) sell (D) saleable

[해석] 2013년 7월 24일자 와인 스펙테이터에는 "무역분쟁이 유럽산 와인의 중국에 대한 매상고를 위협하다"는 기사가 실려 있다.

[해설] 빈 칸에 들어갈 말은 '매상고'라는 의미의 명사로서 wine과 연결된 복합명사다. 먼저 (C)는 동사, (D)는 형용사이기 때문에 탈락, (A)는 판매 행위 자체에 초점을 둔 말이며, (B)는 '매상고(명사)'라는 의미와 '판매의(형용사)'라는 두 가지 의미가 있다. 그러므로 기사의 의미는 무역분쟁이 판매 자체를 위협한다기보다는 분쟁으로 매상이 줄어들 수 있다는 의미를 담고 있다.

정답 I B

4. Unless you complete your term-paper by __________, you will be criticized by your professor.

(A) you (B) yourself

(C) yours (D) your

[해석] 네가 스스로 학기말 과제물을 완성하지 않는다면, 너는 선생님으로부터 비난을 받을 거야.

[해설] 우선 전치사 by 뒤에 올 수 없는 것들을 대입해 보면, (A)는 주어가 you로서 같은 사람이므로 어색하다. 예컨대, 노래 가사에서 I'll stand by you(내가 너를 지켜줄게)는 가능하다. (C)는 '너의 것'을 의미하는 소유대명사이므로 '스스로' 동작을 할 수 없다. (D)는 소유격이므로 문법적으로 틀린 표현이다. 그러므로 (B)의 재귀대명사 yourself를 사용하여 '혼자서, 스스로'의 의미가 되도록 해야 한다. 재귀대명사는 동작의 결과가 동작의 주체에게 뒤돌아가는 것을 의미한다.

정답 I B

5. Nobody really knows exactly how many languages there are in the world, because of the difficulty of distinguishing between a language and the sub-languages or dialects within __________.

(A) that (B) this

(C) it (D) those

[해석] 이 세상에 얼마나 많은 언어들이 있는지 아무도 정확하게 아는 사람이 없다. 왜냐하면 그 안에 있는 언어들, 하위(sub-) 언어들, 그리고 방언들을 구분하기 어렵기 때문이다.

[해설] '~의 안에'의 의미를 가진 전치사 within(= with+in)은 복합전치사라고 하며, '~의 밖에(without, outside)'의 반대의 개념으로 사용된다. 문장에서는 'within+목적어'의 형태로 사용되는 경우가 많다. 빈 칸에는 들어갈 단어는 'it'인데, 이것은 앞 문장의 부사구 'in the world'에서 'world'를 지칭하는 대명사로서 전치사 within의 목적어 역할을 하고 있다. 나머지 (A), (B), (D) 지시대명사들은 대개 문장의 맨 앞에 놓여서 주어의 역할을 하기도 하고, 명사 앞에 놓여 형용사의 기능을 한다.

정답 I C

6. **Of the two suggestions proposed by staff members, this one is more reasonable in terms of appropriateness than ___________.**

(A) other (B) others

(C) the other (D) the others

[해석] 직원들이 건의한 두 제안 중, 타당성이라는 점에서 이것이 다른 것보다 더 합리적이다.

[해설] 일반적으로 두 가지를 비교해 볼 때 첫 번째 것은 대명사 '이것 (this) one'으로, 두 번째는 '다른 것 the other'으로 지칭한다. '다른'의 의미를 가진 (A)와 (B)는 정관사 the 없이 쓰이는 경우는 명사 앞에 놓여서 형용사로 쓰인다.

정답 I C

Exercise

'나파벨리(Napa Valley)'라는 캘리포니아의 와인지구를 아시나요?
그 한가운데에 들어선 친환경 고급호텔인 Bardessono를 둘러볼까요?
Bardessono, Yountille, CA, USA(www.bardessono.com)

LEED Platinum Certified: One of only 3 hotels in the U.S.
[출처] https://bardessono.com/about-bardessono-yountville-california/gallery/

Hotel
convention
English

호텔컨벤션영어

UNIT 3

Taking Phone Calls and Messages

Hotel
convention
English

호텔컨벤션영어

Dialogue

1.

Reception: Good morning. Marriott Seoul. Anna speaking. Can I help you?

Guest: I'd like to speak to Mrs. Choi in room 507, please.

Reception: One moment and I'll connect you, sir.

Guest: Thank you.

Reception: I'm sorry, there's no answer from room 507. Can I take a message for you?

Guest: Yes, please. My name is Jivagoh, Dr. Jivagoh. Please tell her there's a meeting tomorrow at ten o'clock.

Reception: Certainly, sir.

Notes

message n.

① 전갈, 전하는 말, 전언

② 통신(문), 서신, 전보

ex) a verbal message 전언 ↔ a text message 문자 메시지

take a message 메시지를 받다 ↔ leave a message 메시지를 남기다

2.

Reception: Grand Intercontinental, Emily speaking. Can I help you?

Guest: Could I reserve a parking space for tomorrow, please?

Reception: Just one moment. Who's calling, please?

Guest: Ms. Sonia.

Reception: Thank you, Ms. Sonia. You're through now.

3.

Reception: Grand Hotel reservations, Gabriella speaking. Can I help you?

Guest: I'd like to make a room reservation.

Reception: Hello? The line is very bad. Can you speak up a little, please?

Guest: I'd like to make a room reservation for three nights from September the....

Reception: I'm sorry, I didn't catch the date. September...?

Guest: September the 4th. a double room for three nights.

Reception: What name is it?

Guest: Baker. Mr. Baker

Reception: All right sir. And can I have your phone number?

Guest: The country code is 90. Then 216 877 0543.

Reception: Could you repeat that, please?

Guest: 90 216 877 0543

Reception: Thank you. Have a nice day, sir.

Notes

catch vt.
파악하다, 이해하다, (소리를)알아듣다

code n.
① 법전
② 규약, 규칙
③ 신호법, 암호, 약호
④ (컴퓨터)코드, 부호

Vocabulary

Write the word that best completes each sentence.

customary, busboy, decaf, beverage, chef

1. A ________________ is something you drink.

2. We simply call 'decaffeinated coffee' as ________________.

3. The 'usual' or 'normal' thing to do is ________________.

4. The person who prepares meal in a restaurant is the ________________.

5. The ________________ clears and wipes the table after the diners have left.

Global Countries and Culture

Spain
Sevilla

스페인을 생각하면 플라멩코 춤, 투우, 타파스 바(tapas bar) 등의 이미지를 떠올리게 된다. 안달루치아의 세빌리아는 스페인 최고의 플라멩코(flamenco)의 도시이다.

Sevilla was Europe's gateway to the New World in the 16th century. It flourished during the Age of Discovery. The explorers Christopher Columbus, Ferdinand Magellan, and Amerigo Vespucci all sailed from right here.

The Golden Tower was the starting and ending point for trade with the New World. For centuries part of the city's fortifications, it came with a heavy chain draped across the river to protect the harbor. In the 16th century, Sevilla's Golden Age was powered by New World riches.

In the 17th century, all that money made the city an important center of arts and culture. In the 18th century — as its harbor silted up and the Spanish empire crumbled — Sevilla's power faded. And in the 19th century, the once-powerful-now-quaint Sevilla became an important stop on the Romantic-era "Grand Tour of Europe."

In the 20th century, 1992 to be exact, Sevilla hosted a World's Fair that left the city with today's striking 21st-century infrastructure: dramatic bridges, a sleek new train system, and even a new airport. Today, with 700,000 people, it's Spain's fourth-largest city…an exuberant Andalusian capital.

But the charm of Sevilla is best enjoyed in its traditions — like flamenco. Spaniards consider Andalucia the home of flamenco. While impromptu flamenco still erupts spontaneously in Old World bars, most tourists attend a show like this. The men do most of the machine-gun footwork. The women concentrate on graceful turns and a smooth, dramatic step. Flamenco guitarists, with their lightning-fast finger-roll strums, are among the best in the world.

[출처] https://www.ricksteves.com

TOEIC Tips

1. **The particular measures which can attract customers for our hotel __________ based on a typically Korean way of thinking suggested by our management.**

(A) are (B) being

(C) is (D) has been

[해석] 우리 호텔을 찾는 고객들을 끌 수 있는 특별대책은 우리 경영진이 제안한 전형적인 한국식 발상에 근거를 두고 있다.

[해설] 이 문장은 be동사를 찾아 주어의 단·복수에 맞추어 완성하는 문제이다. 즉 주어 measures+be based on(…에 근거를 두다)의 구조로 되어있으므로 be의 자리에 are가 와야 한다. 관계대명사 which 이하 형용사절은 선행사인 measures를 수식한다. (B) being는 분사, (C) is는 단수, (D) has been은 주어가 단수로서 현재완료시제에서 각각 사용하므로 모두 틀린다.

정답 I A

2. **The number of participants __________ that 2013 Korean Food Festivals in Lotte Hotel Seoul hosted by Korea Tourism Organization was immensely successful.**

(A) indicate (B) indicates

(C) express (D) have expressed

[해석] 수많은 참석자들은 한국관광공사가 롯데호텔에서 주최한 2013 한국음식 축제가 매우 성공적이었음을 나타내고 있다.

[해설] 이 문장의 주어 number는 단수형 동사를 취한다는 것이 핵심이다. 즉 the number of 복수명사+단수동사의 구조로 되어있다. (A) indicate(나타내다, 표시하다)와 (C) express(나타내다, 표현하다)는 둘 다 복수형 주어일 때 사용한다. (D)는 현재완료시제이므로 단순과거시제와 같이 한 문장 안에서 쓸 수 없다.

정답 I B

3. **The over-consumption of fossil fuels as well as the rapid urbanization __________. the main reason for the global warming.**

(A) is (B) are

(C) has been (D) have been

[해석] 급속한 도시화뿐만 아니라 화석연료의 과다사용은 지구온난화의 주요한 이유이다.
[해설] 상관접속사 B as well as A (= not only A but also B)의 용법에 관한 문제이다. 이 상관접속사는 둘 중에서 어느 한 쪽을 더 강조하고자 할 때 사용하며, 강조하고자 하는 것이 주어가 된다. 즉 B가 주어가 되며 술어동사 또한 주어의 단·복수에 맞추어야 된다. 이 문장에서는 fossil fuels가 주어가 되므로 동사는 복수형인 (B) are가 된다. (A)는 단수 주어일 때, (C)와 (D)는 문장의 의미가 사실에 입각한 현상을 나타내므로 현재완료시제를 사용할 만한 근거가 없으므로 틀린다. 정답 I B

4. **Recently, paper documents have been used by a lot of companies or government organizations __________ with electronic documents.**

(A) replaced (B) have replaced
(C) have been replaced (D) have been being replaced

[해석] 최근 많은 회사나 정부기관들에 의해서 사용되어온 종이서류들이 전자서류로 대체되고 있는 중이다.
[해설] 이 문장은 서두에 부사 recently가 쓰였으므로 현재완료시제가 되며, 주어 paper documents는 스스로 동작을 하지 못하기 때문에 수동형이 되어야 한다. 아울러 불명확한 어느 시점부터 동작이 시작되어 현재도 진행 중에 있으므로 현재완료수동진행형이어야 한다. (A)는 단순과거이므로 시제가 맞지 않고, (B)는 현재완료시제로서 목적어가 필요하고, (C)는 현재완료수동형으로 정답이 될 수도 있다. 그러나 어느 시점부터 어떤 일이 현재까지 진행되어 왔음을 강조하자면 (D)를 선택하는 것이 옳다. 정답 I B

5. **The all staff members of the hotel are strongly and regularly __________ by the CEO to participate in the job education and training program.**

(A) encouraged (B) encouraging
(C) being encouraging (D) have been encouraged

[해석] 그 호텔의 전직원들은 직무교육에 참여하도록 최고경영자에 의하여 강하게 그리고 정기적으로 권해진다.
[해설] be+p.p.의 수동태 구문이므로 (A) encouraged가 와야 한다. (B)는 능동형 현재진행형이 되기 때문에 문장의 내용과 맞지 않으며, (C)와 (D)는 be동사가 앞에 있기 때문에 문법적으로 맞지 않는다. 정답 I A

6. **Keeping our hotel Web sites updated daily __________ highly recommended to provide our guests with more new information.**

(A) is (B) are
(C) has (D) have

[해석] 우리 호텔의 웹사이트를 매일 업데이트되도록 유지하는 것은, 우리 호텔을 이용하는 고객들에게 새로운 정보를 제공하기 위해서 매우 권장된다.

[해설] 동명사가 주어일 때 술어동사는 항상 단수가 온다는 것을 알아야 한다. 이 문장은 문맥상 be+p.p.의 수동태 문형이므로 be동사 자리에 놓일 단수동사를 찾으면 된다. 주어로서 동명사 keeping은 5형식의 불완전타동사로서 목적어와 목적격보어를 갖는다. (C)는 복수형, (B)와 (D)는 현재완료시제이므로 쓸 수 없다. 즉 have / has+recommended이 되는 경우 recommend는 타동사이므로 목적어가 있어야 한다. 부정사구 to provide(…를 제공하기 위하여)는 부사구이다.

정답 I A

Exercise

우리나라 특급호텔인 '비스타 워커힐'(구 W호텔)의 서비스정신은 'Whatever / Whenever Service'라고 합니다. 무슨 의미일까요?

[출처] www.vistawalkerhillseoul.com

Hotel
convention
English

호텔컨벤션영어

UNIT 4

Hotel Service

Hotel
convention
English

호텔컨벤션영어

Dialogue

1.

Operator: Front desk. May I help you?

Guest: Yes. I'd like to get a wake-up call at 7:00.

(Next morning at 8:00 a.m.)

Operator: Good morning. Operator. How can I help you, sir?

Guest: This is Mr. Lee in room 808. I dont' know why, but I never received a wake up call.

Operator: I'm sorry Mr. Lee. You didn't make a request for a wake up call.

Guest: What!!! I made it last night for half past nine.

Operator: Oh, I see the problem. The night operator put down 888.

Guest: Great!!! My plane leaves in 45 minutes. What are you going to do?

Operator: I'm not sure but I'll speak to my manager.

Guest: Hurry up. I really need to talk to the person in charge.

Operator: Relax, sir. My supervisor is a handy man.

Notes

supervisor n.
관리(감독)자, 감시자, 주임

handy a.
① 알맞은, (연장 따위가) 다루기 쉬운
② 편리한, 간편한
③ 능숙한, 솜씨 좋은, 재빠른

2.

Room service: Room service. Can I help you?

Guest: Yes. This is room 506. I'd like to order some scrambled eggs with bacons and a cup of coffee.

Room service: Yes, sir. Will that be all?

Guest: No, Please bring me some ice cubes and water, too.

Room service: Yes, we'll bring them as soon as possible.

3.

Guest: I'd like these clothes cleaned.

Hotel clerk: Please put your laundry in the paper bag and write down the contents of the laundry on it.

Guest: When will it be ready? Can I get them cleaned by tonight?

Hotel clerk: Sure. It'll be ready by 7 p.m.

Notes

laundry n.
(집합적) 세탁물
coin laundry
동전투입식 세탁기

4.

Guest: The front desk told me to ask you for sightseeing advice.

Concierge: Of course. I'd be more than happy to help. I am, after all, the hotel's concierge.

Guest: Concierge? What exactly is that?

Concierge: We assist you on everything during your stay here in the hotel, from advising where to visit and eat in the city to searching tickets to concerts or airplanes.

Guest: Great! So where should I start my sightseeing?

Concierge: The Statue of Liberty is always a good place to begin.

Guest: I saw the Statue of Liberty on my last visit here. Can you recommend somewhere else?

Concierge: Hmm. What type of interests do you have?

Guest: In my spare time, I really like to view art and go running.

Concierge: Aha! Have you been to Central Park or the Museum of Modern Art?

Guest: No, but I've heard a lot about both.

Concierge: Well, Central Park is wonderful for running. Afterwards, you should head to the Museum to enjoy the art.

Guest: That sounds great. Thanks a lot.

Concierge: I'm sure you'll have a good time there.

Notes

assist v.
① 돕다
② (어떤 일에) 도움이 되다
ex) We will assist you in finding somewhere to live. 당신이 살 곳을 찾도록 우리가 도와주겠다.

assist n.
(스포츠에서) 어시스트[도움주기]

advise v.
① 조언하다, 충고하다, 권고하다
② 자문에 응하다, 고문이 되어주다

advice n.
조언, 충고

Vocabulary

Write the word that best completes each sentence.

housekeeper, travel agent, destination, preference, itinerary

1. The place where you want to go for the trip is your ______________.

2. The ______________ can book your plane reservations.

3. Wanting airline A over airline B is to state your ______________.

4. An ______________ is a day-by-day listing of travel and accommodations.

5. The ______________ cleans the room and makes the bed.

Global Countries and Culture

Spain
The Majesty of Madrid

스페인의 전형적인 '마나나(내일까지 그냥 두라는 의미)'는 이제 사라졌지만, 사람들은 여전히 시계의 지배를 받기보다 사회생활의 필요에 맞추어 일을 하고, 일하는 만큼 즐기는 데도 많은 정력을 쏟는다. 햄의 박물관이라는 이름의 식당을 방문하여 스페인의 특별식인 하몽을 맛본다.

Hi. I'm Rick Steves, back with more of the Best of Europe. This time we're in Madrid — palaces, paseo…and perhaps Europe's finest ham: jamón. Thanks for joining us (...) My Spanish friend and fellow tour guide Carlos Galvin is joining us to share a local's insight into Madrid's culture and food.

Carlos is taking me to a place famous for a food Spaniards are crazy about. If Spain had a national food it would probably be jamón — that's ham.

The eatery, called the Museum of Ham, is tastefully decorated…unless you're a vegetarian, or a pig. This cheap and cheery stand-up bar is an assembly line of meaty treats.

Carlos: Chin Chin!
Rick: Chin Chin! Jamón!
Carlos: Jamón serrano.
Rick: So in Spain you don't just say 'ham'?

Carlos: No, we have different kinds. We've got all those different kinds there. Like for example, jamón granadino, or bellota extra, or Salamanca. You know, the different origins.

Rick: So, what do we have here?

Carlos: So, here we have regular jamón serrano and we have ibérico. This one, the pig has been killed after three months and has been eating just basic pig-food. This one has been eating acorns.

Rick: Acorns?

Carlos: Yeah, they have freedom in the fields and they're eating acorns.

Rick: And this one is much more expensive?

Carlos: Yes, this cost $3, this would cost like $12.

Rick: Can you taste the difference?

Carlos: I can, yes. Oh yes. Here, try.

Rick: Acorns, happy pigs running free in the mountains.

Carlos: That's right.

[출처] https://www.ricksteves.com

TOEIC Tips

1. Strong Orange Pekoe tea is Jennifer's favorite hot drink, even though it ___________ her hinder a good night's sleep.

(A) make (B) makes

(C) has made (D) have made

[해석] 비록 밤에 잠을 설치게 하지만, 진한 오렌지 피코 차는 제니퍼가 가장 좋아하는 더운 음료이다.
[해설] 주절에 대한 종속절로서 양보절을 이끄는 주어 it(= strong Orange Pekoe tea)의 동사를 찾는 문제이다. 이 시제는 '일반적인 사실'을 나타내므로 늘 현재시제를 쓴다. 사역동사 make는 5형식 문형에서 불완전타동사로서 목적어, 목적격보어(원형부정사)를 필요로 한다. 목적격보어 hinder는 make가 사역동사이므로 'to'가 생략된 것이다.
정답 I B

2. Young-sik went to London, took a room in a B&B hotel, and ___________ the following week searching for his brother who came earlier than he did.

(A) had spent (B) spend

(C) spent (D) has spent

[해석] 영식은 런던에 가서 B&B호텔에 방 하나를 잡은 다음, 그보다 조금 일찍 온 동생을 찾는데 일주일을 보냈다.
[해설] 시제의 일치에 관한 문제이다. 주어의 동작이 연속적으로 이어질 때 시제는 변하지 않고 같은 시제가 된다. 그러므로 이 문장에서 동사는 went, took, spent로서 단순과거시제가 연속된다. (A)는 관거완료구문일 때 단순과거보다 한 시제 앞선 시제일 때 사용한다.
정답 I C

3. By 2018, according to the Governor of Gyeonggi Province, the province ___________ the construction of GTX(Great Train Express).

(A) have finished (B) will have finished

(C) will finish (D) will be finished

[해석] 경기도 도지사에 의하면, 2018년까지 경기도는 GTX(광역급행철도)의 건설을 끝마칠 것이다.
[해설] 문장 앞에 by 또는 before가 오고 년, 월, 주와 같은 미래를 나타내는 표현이 나오면 미래완료(will / shall+have+p.p.)시제에 관한 문제이다. (A)는 현재완료, (C)는 미래, 미래수동태이다. 정답 I B

4. **By the time the tourist season starts, the city __________ the road construction project.**

(A) complete (B) will complete

(C) completes (D) will have completed

[해석] 관광 성수기가 시작될 무렵이면 시는 도로공사 프로젝트를 완료했을 것이다.
[해설] 미래완료시제(will have+p.p.)는 미래의 어느 시점까지 계속되어 완료되는 일을 나타낸다. 여기서 〈by the time 주어 현재, 주어+미래 완료(will have+p.p.)〉 시제에 적용한다. 정답 I D

5. **Most manufacturers __________ a revenue decline in the last quarter.**

(A) experience (B) experiences

(C) experienced (D) has experienced

[해석] 제조업자들은 지난분기에 수익감소를 경험했다.
[해설] last quarter(지난분기)가 과거시제를 나타낸다. 정답 I C

6. **The foreman insisted that workers __________ safety helmets while on site.**

(A) wore (B) wears

(C) wear (D) wearing

[해석] 현장 주임은 근로자들이 있을 때는 항상 안전모를 착용해야 한다고 주장했다.
[해설] 제안, 명령, 주장 등의 동사(suggest, recommend, propose, insist, ask, demand, advise) 뒤에 오는 that절에는 '(should)+동사원형'을 쓴다. 정답 I C

Exercise

파리의 리츠호텔을 소개하는 다음의 글을 읽어보세요.

리츠호텔은 세자르 리츠가 1898년에 파리 중심가 방돔광장 15번지에 건립했다. 영국의 에드워드 Ⅶ세를 비롯하여, 소설가 마르셀 프루스트, 대배우 찰리 채플린, 가수 엘튼 존, 패션디자이너 코코 샤넬이 자기 집처럼 드나들었고, 1940년대 파리에 머물던 헤밍웨이는 '천국에 관한 꿈을 꿀 때면 그곳은 언제나 리츠호텔'이라고 말하며 대단한 애정을 드러냈다.

이 호텔에는 헤밍웨이 바가 있는데, 헤밍웨이가 매일저녁 들러서 술을 마신 것에서 붙여진 이름이다. 그 당시 이곳의 바텐더는 헤밍웨이의 친구였다고 한다. 헤밍웨이의 세 번째 부인 Mary가 술을 먹지 못하게 하자, 헤밍웨이는 바텐더 친구에게 술냄새가 나지 않는 칵테일을 개발해달라고 부탁했고, 그 친구는 토마토주스에 독주를 섞으면 술냄새가 나지 않는다는 사실을 발견했고, 그렇게 Bloody Mary가 탄생되었다고 한다.

[출처] www.ritzparis.com

헤밍웨이가 세상을 뜨고 한참 후에 놀랍게도 이곳 리츠호텔 창고에서, 헤밍웨이가 글을 써놓고 잊고 있었던 수사본 12종류가 발견되었다고 한다. 헤밍웨이가 본인의 파리의 집으로 생각하며 묵었던 곳이었음을 말해주는 일화다.

리츠호텔 홈페이지에 들어가면 더 많은 호텔 이야기가 있습니다. 불경기로 객실 점유율이 낮았던 시기에도 500여 명에 이르는 직원들을 유지하며 최고의 서비스를 제공하는 리츠 파리의 명성은 100년이 넘는 세월이 흘렀지만 그대로라는 평을 듣습니다. 리츠호텔에서 일하기 위해서는 4가지 primary qualities를 갖추어야 한다고 합니다. 무엇일까요?

Work at Ritz : Primary qualities of workers in the Hotel:

Discretion

Rigour

Courtesy

Professionalism

UNIT 5

Serving in the Bar

Hotel
convention
English

호텔컨벤션영어

Dialogue

1.

Bartender:	What can I get you, young lady?
Client:	A glass of wine, please.
Bartender:	Red or white?
Client:	White, please. I'd like a very dry wine.
Bartender:	I'm sorry, we don't have any very dry whites, but we do have a nice medium-dry one.
Client:	Well, then, I'll have a beer instead. Do you have any imported beer?
Bartender:	No, I'm sorry, we don't have any imported beer. But we do have some very good local beers like Hite and Cass.
Client:	All right. I'll take Cass.
Bartender:	Will that be all?
Client:	Do you have any snacks or munchies?
Bartender:	Sure. We have nuts and corn chips for free. I'll bring them with your drink.
Client:	Thank you.

Notes

import v.
수입하다 ↔ export
ex) imported beer 수입맥주

munchies n.
(미국속어) 가벼운 음식, 스낵

nut n.
견과(호두, 개암, 밤 따위) [walnut, hazelnut, chestnut]
corn chip n.
(미국) 콘칩(맷돌에 간 옥수수를 반죽하여 튀긴 식품)

2.

Paul:	Let's have a drink here. Come on, here's a table.
Gatsby:	Good idea, Paul. What are you going to have, Mona?
Mona:	Hmm. I think I'll have a cocktail. A Margarita will be good for me. What about you, Gatsby?
Gatsby:	I'll have a gin and tonic.
Paul:	A Margarita, gin and tonic, and a lager beer for me, please.
Waiter:	Would you like draught or bottled?
Paul:	I'll have a large, draught Guinness, please. What about you, Daisy?
Daisy:	Could I have a bottle of San Miguel?
Waiter:	Certainly, ma'am. And would you like ice and lemon in the gin and tonic, sir?
Gatsby:	Yes, please.
Waiter:	Here you are. Shall I charge this to your room?
Paul:	No, thanks. I'll pay cash.
Waiter:	OK. So that's $25.95, sir.
Gatsby:	Why don't we split the bill, pal?
Paul:	Let me pay this time, please.

Notes

gin and tonic

진토닉(진에 토닉워터를 타고 레몬조각을 곁들인 음료)

split v.

① 쪼개다, 쬣다, 째다, 분할하다

② 분배하다, 둘이서 나누다, 분담하다

pal n.

(구어) 동아리, 단짝, 친구, 동료, 여보게, 자네. [SYN → FRIEND]

ex) a pen pal 펜팔

3.

Server:	Anything you need, sir?
Customer:	I think we'll have a pizza with a small bottle of white wine.
Server:	Alright. I'll bring the wine list.
Customer:	And we'd also like to have a pitcher of Coke.
Server:	Sorry, sir. We only have Pepsi.
Customer:	We'd rather have a bottle of mineral water, then.
Server:	No problem, sir.

Notes

pitcher n.

(귀모양의 손잡이와 주둥이가 있는) 물주전자

4.

Sora:	Excuse me. Bartender!
Bartender:	Yes, ma'am, is there anything wrong?

Sora:	Yes, this club soda is very flat. Could you bring me another one, please?
Bartender:	Yes, I'm very sorry about that, ma'am.

Notes

club soda = soda water
(중탄산)소다수, 탄산수

Vocabulary

Write the word that best completes each sentence.

fluctuate, location, benefit, aperitif, rate

1. ________________ is a drink that you have before a meal to whet the appetite.

2. ________________ is taken out to cover costs of an accident.

3. The daily ________________ for a mid-size is $29.99.

4. The ________________ is the place where something is.

5. Prices ________________ depending on the day of the week and time of the year.

Global Countries and Culture

Great Britain
London: Historic and Dynamic

드럼소리에 맞추어 행해지는 근위병 교대식을 출발점으로 시작하여 런던을 둘러본다.

The Changing of the Guard at Buckingham Palace is a fine introduction to London. While no longer ruling a vast empire, London is still a capital of regal traditions. This time-honored ritual still stirs English hearts. And, while you have to be very tall or very early to actually see the guards change, I get a kick out of watching what seems like every tourist in London gathered together in one place at the same time.

Today, England's royal family calls Buckingham Palace home. But for centuries they lived closer to the River Thames, where, in the 11th century, King Edward the Confessor built the first Palace of Westminster. Over the centuries, that palace evolved to become this building and an icon of modern democracy.

Eventually, representatives of local communities — or "commons" — gathered here to be near their king. They began meeting independently as the "House of Commons." And to this day, Britain is ruled from here: the Houses of Parliament.

Visitors are welcome to queue up for a free look at either the uppity House of Lords or the rowdier House of Commons in action.

Like much of the most medieval-looking architecture in Europe, this is actually over-the-top faux medieval. It's Neo-Gothic: built in the 1800s…the Romantic Age.

All across Europe Neo-Gothic was a reaction against the Neoclassical Age of Revolution, which challenged royalty and religion. With this less-cerebral, more romantic style, Victorian England reaffirmed its royal and Christian roots.

People call this famous tower "Big Ben," but it's actually the "Queen Elizabeth Tower." Ben is the 13-ton bell behind the clock.

Here's a fun way to make your sister envious:
Rick: Hi, Jan. It's Rick. Audio postcard from London.

[출처] https://www.ricksteves.com

TOEIC Tips

1. **The 2013 Seoul International Book Fair is expected __________ next week, so interested readers are recommended to go to see the festival.**

(A) to hold (B) hold

(C) to be held (D) holding

[해석] 2013 서울국제도서전이 다음 주에 열릴 것으로 기대되며, 관심 있는 독자들은 전시회를 참관하도록 권해진다.
[해설] 이 문장의 핵심어는 expect이다. 앞 문장에서 expect는 5형식 문형의 형태로서 목적격보어로 수동형의 to-부정사를 취한다. 그런데 형식상으로는 수동태를 취하고 있기 때문에 2형식 문형으로 바뀌었다. (A)는 능동형의 to-부정사, (B)는 현재시제, (D)는 동명사이므로 정답으로 적절치 않다. 정답 I C

2. **The advanced meteorological observation equipments newly introduced allows meteorological observers __________ weather conditions more precisely.**

(A) observe (B) observing

(C) to observe (D) observation

[해석] 새로 도입된 최신형 기상 관측장비는 기상 관측관들이 기상상황을 좀더 정확하게 관측하도록 해준다.
[해설] 이 문장은 5형식 문장에서 사용되는 불완전타동사 allow의 용법에 관한 문제이다. 즉 allow A to do B(A가 B하도록 허용하다)에서 '목적어 A가 목적격보어(to-부정사) B하도록 어떤 여건을 만들어주다'라는 구문이다. 그러므로 빈 칸에는 to-부정사가 와야 한다. equipment와 newly 사이에는 (which are)가 생략되어 있다.
정답 I C

3. **We have decided __________ the deadline for one week.**

(A) extending (B) to extend

(C) extension (D) extensively

[해석] 우리는 마감일을 일주일 연장하기로 결정했다.
[해설] 동사 decide는 to-부정사를 목적어로 취하는 동사이이다. 정답 I B

4. It is important __________ the quality of our product.

(A) improving (B) improve

(C) improvement (D) to improve

[해석] 우리 제품의 품질을 개선하는 것은 중요하다.
[해설] 가주어 it의 진주어인 to V가 와야 한다.

정답 | D

5. Please feel free __________ us if you find this change unsatisfactory.

(A) to call (B) calling

(C) to be called (D) being called

[해석] 만약 이런 변경이 불만스러우시면 주저하지 말고 전화하세요.
[해설] fee free to 부정사 '주저하지 말고 …하다'에 의미를 갖고 있다.

정답 | A

6. The tour conductor reminded all the visitors __________ in the lobby by 7a.m.

(A) is (B) are

(C) being (D) to be

[해석] 여행 인솔자는 모든 방문객들에게 오전 7시까지 로비로 모이라고 재공지했다.
[해설] 구문 'remind A to V(A에게 …할 것을 상기시키다)'에 알맞은 표현이다.

정답 | D

Exercise

아래 글은 영국 런던의 대표적인 호텔인 Savoy호텔을 소개하고 있습니다.

사보이호텔(www.savoylondon.com)은 영국의 에드워디언시대 건축양식과 고풍스러운 아르 데코 형식의 인테리어가 환상적 하모니를 연출하는 럭셔리호텔이다. 268개의 객실을 보유하고 있고, 최신식 시설을 갖추고 있으며, 런던 시내와 템즈강이 한눈에 들어오는 호텔 view는 사보이호텔의 가장 큰 장점 중 하나이다. 특별 제작된 Personality Suite 객실은 Winston Churchill, Maria Callas, Claude Monet, Charlie Chaplin, Katharine Hepburn 등의 이름으로 불리고, Royal Suite 객실은 투 베드룸으로 개조하여 더 넓고 편안하게 사용할 수 있으며, Royal Suite 이용 시에는 개인요리사를 동반하고 여행하는 손님을 위하여 service kitchen이 포함되어 있고, 비서 없이 여행하는 손님을 위하여 사보이 버틀러가 24시간 대기하고 있다.

이 호텔의 큰 특징 중의 하나가 Afternoon Tea라고 하는데, 설명해 보세요.

[출처] www.fairmont.com/savoy-london

UNIT 6

Taking Orders in the Restaurant

Hotel
convention
English

호텔컨벤션영어

Dialogue

1.

Waiter: May I help you?

Lisa: A table for two please.

Waiter: This way.
Are you ready to order?

Lisa: Yes, we'll have the chicken with vegetables and the Shanghai pasta, please.

Waiter: Anything to drink?

Lisa: Just some water please.

(after the meal)

Waiter: Can I get you anything else? Coffee? Dessert?

Lisa: No, just the bill please.

2.

Waiter: May I take your order?

Guest: I'd like a grilled cheese sandwich.

Waiter: And what would you like to drink?

Guest: A glass of Coke, please.

(After the meal)

Waiter: Can I bring you anything else?

Guest: No thank you. Just the bill.

Waiter: Certainly.

Guest: I don't have my glasses. How much is the lunch?

Waiter: That's $6.75.

Guest: Here you are. Thank you very much.

Waiter: You're welcome. Have a good day.

Guest: Thank you, the same to you.

3.

Waiter: Good afternoon, ma'am. Do you have a reservation?

Guest: Yes, in the name of Stevens. I'm staying at the hotel

Waiter: Yes, here we are. A table for one at twelve o'clock. Let me take your coat. Now, there's a table near the window or one out on the terrace. Which one would you prefer?

Guest: It's rather cold today. So I think I'll stay inside.

Waiter: Very well, Mrs. Stevens. Let me show you to your table. Here is the menu. Let me tell you about today's special. The fish of the day is snapper and the soup is chicken noodle.

Guest: Well, I'll have the steak.

Waiter: How would you like that cooked?

Guest: Medium rare, please.

Waiter: Would you like to order some wine?

Guest: Yes, half a bottle of red wine, the Cabernet Sauvignon. I also would like to have a bottle of sparkling water.

Waiter: Okay. Half a bottle of red wine and a bottle of sparkling water. They'll be coming out soon.

Notes

sparkling a.

불꽃을 튀기는, 번쩍하는, 거품이 이는(opp. still)

still a.

정지한, 움직이지 않는, 소리가 없는 조용한, 거품이 일지 않는

ex) Sit still! 가만히 앉아 있어라!

Still waters run deep. (속담)잔잔한 물이 깊은 법.

Vocabulary

Write the word that best completes each sentence.

brochures, weight room, hotbed, manager, winery

1. If you need to do your workout we have a _______________ on the third floor.

2. A _______________ is where grapes are turned into alcoholic beverages.

3. The wide range of activities here makes it a tourist _______________.

4. I'll let you voice your complaint about the rate to the hotel _______________.

5. If you've never been to this city, you should take a look at our _______________.

Global Countries and Culture

Great Britain
London: Mod and Trad

런던에서 가장 유명한 백화점인 Harrods를 둘러보고 대영박물관의 Great Court로 가서 칼 마르크스, 마하트마 간디, 조지 버나드 쇼가 즐겨 찾던 서재의 분위기를 느껴본다.

Harrods is London's vast and venerable department store. It's huge — 300 departments, a million square feet on seven floors — yet classy. The food halls with their Edwardian tiled walls, delicious displays, tempting eateries, and staff in period costumes are lots of fun.

A small shrine invites visitors to pay their respects to Princess Diana and Dodi Al Fayed — whose father owns Harrods.

The Egyptian Escalator is a reminder that Mr. Al Fayed is from Egypt, and he spent a fortune revitalizing this historic department store. Riding it, you ascend into Harrods shopping wonderland. You'll find everything from sprawling halls of designer women's wear to traditional men's wear, to a $12,000 mini Jaguar — for the kid who has everything.

Huge European cities like London are made manageable by excellent subway systems. London's mighty "Tube" takes us anywhere in the center for less than the cost of a cucumber sandwich at Harrods. We're on our way to the British Museum.

At the peak of its empire, when the Union Jack flew over a quarter of the planet, England collected art and artifacts as fast as it collected colonies. This place, the British Museum, is the showcase for those extraordinary treasures.

Its centerpiece is the Great Court — an impressive example of Europe's knack for preserving old architectural spaces by making them fresh, functional, and inviting. The stately Reading Room — a temple of knowledge and high thinking — was the study hall for Oscar Wilde, Rudyard Kipling, and T.S. Eliot. Karl Marx researched right here while writing Das Kapital.

[출처] https://www.ricksteves.com

TOEIC Tips

1. Soo-jin has lived in Beijing since the year before last and she is still getting used to __________ to the Beijing dialect of Mandarin Chinese.

(A) listen (B) listening

(C) be listened (D) be listening

[해석] 수진은 재작년부터 북경에서 살고 있는데, 여전히 북경 방언인 만다린 중국어를 듣는 것에 익숙해지고 있다(아직도 완전히 익숙한 것은 아니다).

[해설] 이것은 'get used to ~ing(~에 익숙해지다)'의 구문을 활용한 문장이다. 즉 'get used to' 다음에는 동명사가 온다는 것을 알면 쉽게 맞힐 수 있는 문제이다. 정답 I B

2. The marketing director of our hotel suggested __________ our promotional strategy to attract Southeast Asian tourists who want to experience the Korean Wave.

(A) reexamine (B) reexamining

(C) to reexamine (D) reexamination

[해석] 우리 호텔의 홍보이사는 한류를 체험하고 싶어하는 동남아관광객들의 관심을 끌기 위한 우리의 홍보전략을 재검토할 것을 제안했다.

[해설] 이 문장의 핵심어는 suggest이며 목적어로 동명사를 취한다. (A) 동사는 suggest가 있으므로 불가, (C)는 부정사이기 때문에 불가, (D)는 명사로 뒤에 오는 명사구 our promotional strategy와의 연결고리(대개는 전치사)가 없으므로 쓸 수 없다 정답 I B

3. Our hotel has been committed to __________ the good and great service in the hospitality to our guests for the past 15 years.

(A) provide (B) provided

(C) providing (D) provision

[해석] 저희 호텔은 지난 15년 동안 고객에 대한 환대에 있어서 최고의 서비스를 제공하는데 헌신해 왔습니다.
[해설] 이 문장은 'be committed to+~ing(동명사) : ~에 헌신하다'를 활용한 구문이다. 관용적으로 사용되는 이러한 표현들은 문장을 통째로 암기하는 것이 좋다. (B)는 문법적으로 맞지 않고, (A)는 'to'와 연결하여 부정사구로 착각할 수 있다. (D)는 뒤에 명사구가 오므로 쓸 수 없다. 정답 I C

4. **Those employees (particularly chefs) ___________ in the kitchen of a hotel must always wear a toque (traditional hat) and white double-breasted jacket.**

(A) work (B) are working
(C) worked (D) working

[해석] 호텔 주방에서 일하는 직원(특히 요리사)들은 늘 토크(챙 없는 모자)와 양쪽에 단추 달린 흰 재킷을 입어야 한다.
[해설] 이 문장의 주어는 employees이고, 동사는 must wear이다. 그러므로 빈칸에는 employees를 수식하는 'working (일하는)'을 의미하는 능동형의 분사가 와야 한다. 즉 'employees (who are) working in the kitchen'에서 ( ) 안에 있는 것이 생략된 형태이다. (A)는 뒤에 동사가 있으므로 쓸 수 없고, (B)는 관계대명사 who가 있어야 되며, (C)는 관계사 앞에 오는 선행사가 사물일 때 수동의 의미로 쓰일 수 있다. 정답 I D

5. **In many countries, families live in the same villages from generation to generation, ___________ the structure of traditional family life.**

(A) preserve (B) preserving
(C) preserved (D) preservation

[해석] 많은 나라에서 가족들은 대를 이어 같은 마을에서 살며, 전통적인 가족구조를 보존한다.
[해설] 두 문장의 주어가 같을 때 접속사(and)를 생략하고 대신 두 문장 중 한 문장의 동사를 분사의 형태로 만들어 두 문장을 하나의 문장으로 묶는 것을 분사구문이라고 한다. 즉 빈칸에 preserving(= and (families) preserve)로 처리함으로써 복잡한 중문이 단문으로 간결하게 되는 것이다. 정답 I B

6. **According to the recent poll, it is significantly important to make new guests ___________ in the hospitality industry such as hotels.**

(A) satisfy (B) satisfying
(C) satisfaction (D) satisfied

[해석] 최근 여론조사에 의하면, 호텔과 같은 환대산업에서 신규고객을 만족시키는 것이 지극히 중요하다.

[해설] 이 문장은 … it is~ to의 강조구문이다. 즉 to 이하(진주어)가 it(가주어)와 같은 의미를 갖는다. 5형식문을 만드는 사역동사 make는 목적어 new guests가 목적격보어(형용사)가 되도록 하는 역할을 하는데, 목적격보어로는 '~이 되도록'의 의미를 가진 수동형 형용사(과거분사)가 와야 한다. 목적격보어가 될 수 있는 형용사로는 (B)와 (D)인데 목적어가 동작을 받는 수동형 형용사는 과거분사형이다. 정답 I D

Exercise

세계에서 가장 아름다운 일몰을 볼 수 있다고 자랑하는 그리스의 산토리니에 위치한 Dreams Luxury Suites호텔을 아시나요? 그곳에서 고객들에게 제공하는 서비스들입니다. 해석해 볼까요?

- Reception with concierge assistance
- "Tailor made services" prior to arrival
- All suites with Caldera sea view
- Each room individually designed and furnished
- Private fresh water swimming pools
- Private fresh water Jacuzzi
- Private candlelight dinners
- Welcome drink and cold towels upon arrival
- Complimentary Room service with American breakfast
- Candle light and rose petals room decoration on request
- Twice daily maid service
- Laundry&dry cleaning services

이 호텔에서 제공하는 패키지 중에서 150유로의 가장 저렴한 상품과 700유로의 비싼 상품을 한 번 비교해 볼까요?

"SUNSET" – 150 euro per suite / per stay

- One bottle of sparkling wine on arrival
- Rose Petals and Candle Light Decoration in Suite
- One Candlelight Dinner on your terrace

"DREAMS OF ULTIMATE ROMANCE" – 700€ per suite / per stay

- VIP Transportation from and to Airport or Port
- Moet Champagne on arrival
- Rose Petals and Candle Light Decoration in Suite
- Satin bed sheets to celebrate your first night
- One Candlelight Dinner on your terrace
- One bottle of Santorinian Wine
- Car Rental for 2 days
- Romantic sunset cruise around Volcano and Caldera's Cliffside
- One relaxing 60' min massage treatment per person
- Bathrobes with Hotel's logo as your memento

[출처] www.travel-pictures-gallery.com

Hotel
convention
English

호텔컨벤션영어

UNIT 7

Dealing with Requests

Hotel
convention
English

호텔컨벤션영어

Dialogue

1.

Receptionist:	Good evening. Reception. Tina speaking. What can I do for you?
Guest:	Good evening. My name is Mary Taylor. I'm in room 310. I've just checked in.
Receptionist:	Yes, Miss Taylor.
Guest:	There's a problem with the air conditioning. I can't turn it down and it's freezing in here.
Receptionist:	I'm sorry, I'll have it checked for you right away.
Guest:	That's not all. The bathroom hasn't been cleaned.
Receptionist:	I'm so sorry, it should have been cleaned by now. I'll call Maintenance and have it cleaned for you right away.
Guest:	Also, can you do something about the television? There's a picture but no sound.
Receptionist:	Sure, I'll call Maintenance and have it fixed or replaced immediately. I am very sorry about this, ma'am. I'll see to these matters right now.

Notes

see to

~에 주의하다, 일 따위를 맡다, ~을 처리하다, ~을 준비하다

ex) I'll see to that. 그건 내가 맡아 처리하겠다.

2.

Receptionist: Hello. Reception. May I help you?

Guest: Yes, I hope so. I can't find my room key.

Receptionist: Oh, what room are you in?

Guest: Room 707.

Receptionist: That's all right. Just come to Reception and I'll give you another one.

Guest: Thank you very much.

3.

Guest: A colleague left a message for me at the reception last night but nobody gave it to me.

Receptionist: I'm sorry. I'll look into it.

Guest: Another thing. The people in the room next door are making a lot of noise. Can I change the room?

Receptionist: I'm awfully sorry about the inconvenience. I'll see what I can do.

Notes

inconvenience n.

불편(한 것), 부자유, 폐(가 되는 일), 성가심

ex) It is no inconvenience to me. 조금도 불편하지 않다.

If it's no inconvenience to you. 폐가 되지 않는다면.

4.

Guest:	I forgot my room number.
Receptionist:	May I have your name, please?
Guest:	It's Ho-young Kim.
Receptionist:	Mr. Kim, you're in room 1818.
Guest:	1880?
Receptionist:	No, eighteen eighteen, not eighteen eighty.
Guest:	Oh, I see. What floor is it on?
Receptionist:	It's on the 18th floor, sir.
Guest:	I understand. Where are the elevators?
Receptionist:	Turn right at the coffee shop. The elevators are in front of you.
Guest:	Turn right at the copy shop?
Receptionist:	Oh, no! I'll have the bellboy show you to your room.
Guest:	Thank you so much. You're very kind.
Receptionist:	My pleasure, sir.

Vocabulary

Write the word that best completes each sentence.

amuesment, draw, frustrating, suburbs, newlyweds

1. Two people who have just been married are ______________.

2. An ______________ is an event specially designed to draw people to it.

3. To attract or lure many people is to ______________ them.

4. When a traffic jam is very bad and I can't get where I want to go, it is ______________.

5. The opposite of moving into the city is moving to the ______________.

Global Countries and Culture

Belgium and the Netherlands
Bruges and Brussels

벨기에 사람들은 초콜릿의 미식가들이다. 그래서인지 시내 도처에서 발견되는 초릿렛 가게에서는 백 가지가 넘는 다양한 맛의 초콜릿을 볼 수 있다. 쿠바산 시가의 향을 지닌 초콜릿에 이르기까지.

The people of Bruges are connoisseurs of fine chocolate. You'll be tempted by chocolate-filled display windows all over town. Locals buy their chocolates fresh daily — like other people buy pastries. They love the family-run places like Dumon, where Madame Dumon and her children are hard at work. Their ganache, a dark creamy combo, wows chocoholics.

Bruges seems to have a chocolate shop on every corner — and some are more adventurous than others. The Chocolate Line — famous for its many "gastronomic" varieties — proudly shows off its kitchen. Everything here is lovingly made by hand. Some specials come with an extra dose of creativity.

Rick: So, how many different flavors do you have?
Clerk: About 60 different kinds, we have.
Rick: 60! What are some interesting…you must have some special flavors?
Clerk: We have special ones like Cuban tobacco, or saffron curry, or ginger.
Rick: Cuban tobacco? Is that legal for Americans?

Clerk: Yes.

Rick: Can I try one?

Clerk: Yeah, sure sir.

Rick: So how is this made?

Clerk: It's a layer of marzipan, flavored by a tobacco of Cuba.

Rick: Cuban tobacco leaves? Wow! It's probably not as good as a Cuban cigar, but it's very good for chocolate. (...)

My favorite way to explore Bruges is on two wheels. Just about anywhere in Europe, where the biking's good, you'll find handy and inexpensive bike rentals. Get lost on the back streets, away from the shopping and the tour groups.

[출처] https://www.ricksteves.com

TOEIC Tips

1. After completing the report, the deputy manager Kim locked the door of his office __________ he left the office building.

(A) or (B) and

(C) but (D) nor

[해석] 보고서를 완성한 후, 김 대리는 사무실 문을 잠그고 회사건물을 떠났다.
[해설] 대등한 두 개의 문장을 한 문장으로 만들자면 등위접속사를 사용하여 연결하면 되는데, 이 문장에서는 동작이 순차적으로 이어지는 것을 의미하는 and가 가장 적당하다.
정답 I B

2. __________ the extra hours of daylight affect was sufficient last year, the grapevines still did not produce a high yield in California.

(A) Although (B) Due to

(C) Since (D) However

[해석] 지난해 일조량이 충분했음에도 불구하고, 캘리포니아의 포도나무들은 여전히 높은 생산량을 내지 못했다.
[해설] 양보의 부사절에서 접속사를 찾는 문제이다. 양보절이란 두 개의 절(부사절+주절)이 대립 또는 대조를 이룰 때 주로 사용하는 절이다. 위의 문장의 경우에 '~하였지만, ~하지 못했다'의 구문으로 양보절을 이끄는 접속사는 '비록~하지만(although, though, even if, even though)'의 의미를 나타내는 접속사를 필요로 한다. (B)와 (C)는 '~때문에'를, (D)는 '그러나'를 의미한다.
정답 I A

3. Recently, most of the people want to know __________ manufactured foodstuffs from factories contain harmful ingredients or not.

(A) that (B) whether

(C) even if (D) though

[해석] 최근 대부분의 사람들은 공장에서 제조된 식료품들이 유해성분을 포함하고 있는지 아닌지를 알고 싶어 한다.
[해설] 본동사 want의 목적절을 이끄는 명사절 접속사를 찾아내는 문제이다. (C)와 (D)는 양보의 부사절을 이끄는 접속사들이므로 쓸 수 없고, (A)와 (B) 둘 다 명사절을 이끄는 접속사이긴 하지만, 문장의 맨 뒤에 'or not'이 있으므로 'whether A or B(A인지 B인지)'의 의미를 가진 명사절 접속사가 와야 한다.
정답 I B

4. **Recently, the hotel hired two experienced employees, all of ________ had worked in disaster prevention as well as fire fighting facilities.**

(A) them (B) which
(C) that (D) whom

[해석] 최근 그 호텔은 소방 및 방재분야에서 일한 경험이 있는 두 명의 경력직 직원을 채용했다.
[해설] 빈칸에 들어갈 말은 of의 목적어가 되면서 동시에 선행사 employees를 수식하는 관계대명사(앞 문장과 뒤 문장을 연결하는 접속사의 역할)가 와야 한다. (A)는 접속사의 기능이 없는 단순한 목적격 대명사이다. (B) which는 선행사가 사물일 때 사용되며, (C)는 선행사가 사람과 사물 둘 다 쓸 수 있지만, 여기서는 employees가 복수형이므로 불가하다.

정답 I D

5. **This pair of designer shoes should be kept in a dry place ________ temperature extremes are minimal.**

(A) which (B) that
(C) where (D) who

[해석] 이 명품구두는 온도차이가 최소화 된 건조한 곳에 보관하는 것이 바람직하다.
[해설] 선행사가 어떤 장소를 나타내며, 이것이 어떤 곳인지를 수식하는 관계부사를 찾는 문제이다. (A)는 사물, (B)는 사물과 사람, (D)는 사람을 각각 선행사로 받는 관계사들이다. 관계사를 접속사로 분류하기도 하는데, 이것은 관계사가 문장과 문장을 연결하는 접속의 기능을 가지기 때문이다. 흔히 조동사 should는 '~해야 한다'는 의무 / 당위성을 나타내는 말로 해석하는 경우가 있으나 실제는 'It's good / right thing to do(~하는 것이 좋다 / 옳다)'의 의미로 더 많이 사용된다는 것도 알아두자.(* Grammar in Use를 참조할 것)

정답 I C

6. **Please proceed to the entrance ________ one of our staff will courteously guide you to the wedding reception.**

(A) which (B) that
(C) where (D) why

[해석] 출입구 쪽으로 곧장 가십시오. 저희 직원이 결혼 피로연장소로 정중하게 안내할 겁니다.
[해설] 관계부사 where의 바로 앞에 놓여서 어떤 장소를 나타내는 문장은 대개 완전한 문장이다. 그러므로 빈칸을 관계사로 채울 때 먼저 앞 문장이 완전한지 아닌지를 따져봐야 한다. (A) which와 (B) that는 관계대명사로서 앞에 오는 선행사를 꾸미는 형용사절을 이끈다. (D) why는 이유나 원인을 나타내는 부사절을 이끄는 관계부사이다.

정답 I C

Exercise

많은 여인들이 5월의 신부를 꿈꾸듯이 또한 많은 아가씨들이 뉴욕의 플라자호텔에서의 결혼식을 소망한다고들 합니다. 이렇게 유명한 플라자호텔의 모든 객실에는 다음과 같은 설비가 갖추어져 있는데요, 한 번 알아볼까요?

[출처] www.theplazany.com

COMMON AMENITIES

All rooms and suites at The Plaza, New York offer the following amenities:

- Beaux Arts inspired décor and chandeliers
- White glove butler service on every floor
- Twice daily housekeeping service
- In-room iPads to control guestroom and suite contour lighting and temperature. It also connects each guest with a vast array of hotel services.

- High Speed Internet Access(Wireless and wired for $14.95 / 24 hrs; Complimentary for Fairmont President's Club members)
- Sophisticated telephone and networking technology
- Wall mounted flat screen televisions
- Exquisite inlaid "earth stone" mosaic tiled bathroom, most with glass shower and bathtub
- 24-carat gold plated Sherle Wagner faucets and accessories with hand crafted solid white marble vanities designed exclusively for The Plaza
- 100% cotton finest Italian oversized bath towels and linens
- Lavish terry or light weight bathrobes
- Signature toiletries by Caudalie
- Hairdryer
- Refrigerated private bar
- 24-hour In-room dining
- Spacious closets
- Suit, skirt and padded hangers
- In-room safe(with electrical outlet)
- DVD player in room
- iLuv Stereo Audio System with clock radio
- Music and video library access
- Iron and ironing board
- Newspapers

UNIT 8

Checking-out

Hotel
convention
English

호텔컨벤션영어

Dialogue

1.

Guest: I'd like to check out please.

Receptionist: What room number?

Guest: Room 231.

Receptionist: That's $250 please.

Guest: Here we go.

Receptionist: Thank you. Sign here please. Have a good journey.

2.

Guest: I'm leaving. Here is my key.

Hotel Clerk: Just one second, sir, and I'll give you your receipt. Here you go.

Guest: Thank you very much.

Hotel Clerk: Sir, did you enjoy your stay here?

Guest: Most of my time here was pleasant. And New York itself is fantastic.

Hotel Clerk: I'm glad you enjoyed the city. Have a good day, sir.

3.

Hotel Clerk: Did you enjoy your stay with us?

Guest: Yes, very much so. However, I now need to get to the airport.

I have a flight that leaves in about two hours. So what is the quickest way to get there?

Hotel Clerk: We do have a free airport shuttle service.

Guest: That sounds great, but will it get me to the airport on time?

Hotel Clerk: Yes, it should. The next shuttle leaves in 15 minutes, and it takes approximately 25 minutes to get to the airport.

Guest: Great. I'll just wait in the lounge area. Will you please let me know when it will be leaving?

Hotel Clerk: Of course, sir. Oh, before you go, would you be able to settle the mini-bar bill?

Guest: Oh yes certainly. How much will that be?

Hotel Clerk: The bill comes to $37.50. How would you like to pay for that?

Guest: I'll pay with my Visa.

Hotel Clerk: Would you like to sign the hotel guestbook while you wait?

Guest: Sure, I had a really good stay here and I'll recommend this hotel to others.

Hotel Clerk: That's good to hear. Thank you again for staying at The Grand Lakewood Hotel.

Notes

receipt n.

① 영수증

② 받기, 수령, 인수

ex) Here are your receipt and change. 여기 영수증과 잔돈이다.

shuttle n.

① (직조기의) 북, (재봉틀의 밑실이 든) 북

② (근거리) 왕복 운행(열차, 버스 따위)

ex) shuttle bus 근거리 왕복 버스

shuttlecock (배드민턴의)셔틀콕, 깃털 공치기 놀이

Vocabulary

Write the word that best completes each sentence.

still, vending machine, outstanding, milk, hot tub

1. If the bill is not paid yet, it's an ______________ bill.

2. There are two kinds of water, sparkling water and ______________ water.

3. After your long conference you can relax in the ______________.

4. I'll call room service and ask them to bring you some fresh ______________.

5. You need coins to get items from the ______________.

Global Countries and Culture

Belgium and the Netherlands
Amsterdam

네덜란드의 화가, 빈센트 반 고흐의 미술관을 찾아본다. 37살의 나이로 권총자살로 생을 마감했는데, 말년에 폭발적인 열정을 보이면서 그의 마지막 70일 동안 그는 70점의 작품을 그렸다. 2017년 가을에 개봉한 〈러빙 빈센트, Loving Vincent〉는 세계 최초로 유화로만 제작된 애니메이션 영화로, 고흐의 많은 명화들을 볼 수 있다. 115명의 화가가 팀을 이루어 수년에 걸쳐 그려낸 것이라고.

An entire museum is dedicated to the work of the great Dutch artist, Vincent van Gogh. The Van Gogh Museum — laid out as a stroll through the story of Vincent's life — shows how intimately his life and art were intertwined.

Van Gogh grew up in poor, rural Holland. From the start, he had an affinity for working people. In paintings like his Potato Eaters — a painting as dark and grainy as the soil itself — he gives these farm laborers the same dignity Rembrandt gave to merchants and aristocrats.

As a young man, Vincent was very religious. He studied to be a pastor and did church work in poor communities. But this wasn't his true calling. He decided to paint, to capture the world he felt so intensely on canvas.

He moved to Paris, and the City of Light opened up a whole new world of color. Vincent hobnobbed with the Impressionists. He studied their bright colors, rough brushwork, and everyday scenes.

He painted shimmering reflections like Monet…café snapshots like Degas…still-lifes like Cézanne…and self-portraits like nobody else. But Vincent longed to strike out on his own. In 1888, he headed for the south of France, arriving just as winter was turning to spring. Energized by the sun-drenched colors and the blue, blue sky, in just two years Vincent produced an explosion of canvases.

His unique style evolved beyond the Impressionists' — thicker paint, brighter colors, and swirling brushwork that made even inanimate objects pulse with life.

Vincent's ecstasy alternated with depression. Eventually, he was admitted to a local hospital. His letters home told of his great loneliness. While in the hospital, he found peace painting calm scenes of nature. But he also wrestled with his inner world, capturing spiritual scenes with surreal colors, twisted forms, and dark outlines.

In this, one of his last works, the canvas is a wall of thick paint, with roads leading nowhere, and ominous black crows taking flight. Overwhelmed with life, Vincent walked into a field like this one…and shot himself.

[출처] https://www.ricksteves.com

TOEIC Tips

1. **Grand Hyatt Cannes Hotel Martinez, one of the most expensive hotel in the world, is ___________ the heart of Cannes, France and one of the prime destinations for exhibitions and conventions.**

(A) next (B) across
(C) near (D) beside

[해석] 세계에서 가장 비싼 호텔의 하나인 깐느 마르티네즈호텔은 프랑스 깐느의 도심 및 박람회 또는 총회의 개최지로서 최고의 명소에서 가까운 곳에 있다.
[해설] 거리를 나타내는 전치사 중에 (A) next (to)와 (D) beside는 '바로 옆에 나란히'라는 방향의 의미를 담고 있고, (B) across는 '가로질러서'를 의미하므로 거리와는 상관없는 표현이다. (C) near는 '가까이에'라는 의미로 방향과는 무관하게 쓰이는 전치사이다. 정답 I C

2. **Hyeon-A has finished her internship at a hotel in Suwon and is working ___________ a new member of the staff in Hotel M in Yeoeuido, Seoul.**

(A) in (B) as
(C) since (D) for

[해석] 현아는 수원에 있는 어떤 호텔에서 인턴십을 마치고, 서울 여의도에 있는 엠호텔에서 신입사원으로 일하고 있다.
[해설] (B) as는 신분을 나타내는 명사구 앞에 놓여서 '~로서' 구체적인 동작의 행위자를 나타낼 때 쓰인다. 전치사 in, for, since는 이 문장의 문맥상 쓸 수 없다. 정답 I B

3. **The baseball game between LA Dodgers and San Diego which was supposed to be held Wednesday evening was canceled ___________ bad weather.**

(A) because (B) despite
(C) due to (D) although

[해석] 수요일 저녁에 열리기로 되어 있었던 엘에이 다저스와 샌 디에고 간의 야구경기는 악천후 때문에 취소되었다.

[해설] 빈칸의 명사구 앞에는 '~때문에'의 의미를 가진 전치사가 와야 한다. 우선 (A)와 (C)가 같은 의미가 있기 때문에 살펴보자면, (A)의 because는 (C)의 due to와 같은 의미를 나타내지만 because는 종속절을 이끄는 접속사이므로 탈락이다. (B)와 (D)는 둘 다 '~에도 불구하고'의 의미로서 이 문장의 문맥과 무관하다: despite는 명사구 앞에 오는 전치사, although는 부사절을 이끄는 접속사이다. 정답 I C

4. Please make sure that making guests ____________ is the most important liability over other responsibilities of our hotel.

(A) satisfaction (B) satisfied

(C) satisfactorily (D) satisfactional

[해석] 고객을 만족시켜야 하는 것은 우리 호텔의 다른 어떤 책무 중에서 가장 중요한 의무라는 것을 명심하기 바란다.

[해설] 문장 형식은 명령문이며 that 이하 목적절에 2형식(S+V+C) 문형을 가진 3형식 복문이다. 즉 (주어)+동사+(that) 목적어 (주어+동사+보어)의 문장 형식인데, 유의할 점은 that 이하 목적절의 주어는 마치 5형식(주어+동사+목적어+보어)의 문장 형식을 취하고 있다는 점이다. 사역동사의 역할을 하는 making의 목적어는 guests이며, 이 목적어의 뒤에서 보어의 역할을 하는 것은 과거분사형의 형용사이다(guests (to be) satisfied). (A) satisfaction(만족)는 명사이므로 올 수 없고, (C) satisfactorily는 부사, (D) satisfactional은 형용사이지만 수동형이 와야 하므로 쓸 수 없다. 정답 I B

5. Le Meridien New Delhi Hotel launched new executive floor, which ___________ it profits of more than a tens of thousands of dollars last year.

(A) brought (B) allowed

(C) generated (D) created

[해석] 르 메리디앙 뉴델리호텔은 귀빈층을 운영하기 시작했는데, 그것은 작년에 수만 달러가 넘는 수익을 가져다주었다.

[해설] 관계대명사 which(접속사(and)+대명사(it))는 앞 문장 전체를 받는다. that 이하는 4형식(주어+동사+간접목적어+직접목적어) 문장으로 되어 있다. 그러므로 주어진 단어 중 4형식 문장에 쓰이는 수여(여격)동사를 찾는 문제이다. (C) generated(…을 야기했다, …을 초래했다)와 (D) created(…을 만들어냈다, …을 창작했다)는 완전타동사로서 3형식 문형에서 사용되고, (B) allowed(…을 허락했다, .…하도록 내버려두었다)는 불완전타동사로서 5형식 문형에서 사용된다. 정답 I A

6. **Some of the waiters have complained that the special instructions of the CEO do not ___________ them wholly.**

(A) repudiate (B) accept

(C) abandon (D) discard

[해석] 몇몇 웨이터들은 최고경영자의 특별지시가 그들에게 전적으로 받아들일 수 없다고 불평했다.

[해설] 3형식 문형에서 that 이하 목적절의 동사를 묻는 문제이다. 문맥상으로 (B) accept(…을 받아들이다)가 맞다. 나머지는 내용과는 정반대의 의미를 가진 단어들이다: (A) repudiate(…을 거부하다, 거절하다), (C) abandon(…를 단념하다, 포기하다), (D) discard(…를 버리다, …을 포기하다)

정답 I B

Exercise

Necker Island의 홈페이지에 들어가면 호텔을 소개하는 짧은 동영상이 있습니다. 섬 통째로 빌릴 수 있는 이 호텔이야말로 여러분의 집(Your home)이고 휴식을 취할 수 있는 곳(Your place to relax)이고, 즐거운 시간을 보낼 수 있는 곳(Your time to play)이라고 소개하면서 마지막에 'The only thing missing is you'로 마무리하고 있습니다. 잘 들어보시고 호텔을 소개하는 문장들을 적어보세요.

[출처] http://www.virginlimitededition.com/en/necker-island/gallery

Hotel
convention
English

호텔컨벤션영어

UNIT 9

For Convention(I)

Hotel
convention
English

호텔컨벤션영어

Presentation

1.

Korea Convention Center를 견학하러 온 사람들에게 시설담당자가 센터를 한 바퀴 돌아보기 전에 이 센터에 관한 안내발표를 하는 상황이다. 발표를 하려면 어떤 표현으로 시작하는 것이 좋을까?

Hello and welcome to the Korea Convention Center. I'm Geoff Maxwell, the Facility Manager in charge of the facility you'll be seeing today. I know some of you have come a long way today so we aim to make your tour both interesting and worthwhile. Before we start the tour, I'd like to give you a brief presentation about the company. This will help to put the service side of the business into context.

My talk will last about 15 minutes and I'll be using the flip chart. Now there's quite a lot to cover, so I'd be grateful if you'd hold any questions until the end of my talk.

As you can see, I've divided up my presentation into three main parts. Firstly, we'll run briefly through the history of the company. Secondly, I'll tell you something about our main activities, this is important in understanding the quality of our services. And finally, I'll come to the people our most important asset.

OK? Let's start with the history. Korea Convention Center started out as a private limited company when it was first established in 1975 ....

[출처] 컨벤션 영어, YoungJin.com

Notes

in charge of ~를 맡고 있는
aim to ~할 목표를 갖고 있다
context 맥락
cover 다루다
grateful 감사한
run through 훑어보다
asset 자산

2.

본인을 소개하고 발표 내용을 전달하는 영어표현을 살펴보자.

A. 컨벤션의 스폰서십을 확보할 전략을 발표한다.

Good morning, ladies and gentlemen. It's a pleasure to be with you today. My name is Mee-Jin Lee and I'm in charge of the Convention Team at our Headquarters here in Seoul, Korea. We are here today to review some key figures and to outline the strategy to secure the sponsorship for the coming Convention. So what I intend to do is to break down this presentation into three sections: first, the financial review; second, the options we have; and finally, the strategy I propose. If you have any questions, please feel free to interrupt me, but I should also say that there will be an opportunity to discuss issues at greater length after my talk.

[출처] 컨벤션영어, YoungJin.com

Notes

It's a pleasure to be with you 여러분과 함께 하게 되어 매우 기쁘다
We are here today 오늘 우리가 여기에 모인 것은 ~이다
key figure 주요 수치
outline 개요를 말하다

feel free to 기꺼이 ~하다
interrupt 중단하다
at greater length: in more dept 좀 더 자세히

B. 컨벤션 캠페인에 대해 발표한다.

Good afternoon and thank you for making the effort to be here with us today. My name's Chang Hyun Lee and I'm responsible for public relations. What I'd like to do today is to talk about our recent campaign for the upcoming Convention. This brief talk will hopefully act as a springboard for discussion. I'm going to look at the Convention campaign from three points of view: firstly, the customers who will participate at the Convention secondly, the Organizing Committee members. And finally your point of view. It may well be different, and we'd like to hear from you.

[출처] 컨벤션영어, YoungJin.com

Notes

making the effort to be here with us 우리와 함께 하고자 노력한 것
public relations PR 홍보
act as a springboard for discussion 토론의 도약대로서 역할을 하다
point of view 관점

Writing Tips

1. 홍보용 편지는 컨벤션과 전시 관련 서비스를 제공하는 회사나 호텔의 선의를 전달하면서 제공할 서비스를 소개하는 편지이다.

July 22, 2003

Mr. Reid Mailtland
American Association of Jewelers
17951 Pearlman Boulevard
Emerald, TX 75222

Re: Convention Services Proposal

Dear Mr. Mailtland

As you know, ICEM Convention Services had the pleasure of submitting a proposal to you this past March. Realizing that you must be reviewing quotes at this time, I wish to express, on behalf of ICEM Convention services, that we are noted for providing exceptional service.
If, in our proposal, you find items that require any additions or alterations which may be necessary, please let me know. We will certainly make every effort to accommodate your requests. We hope that we will be a strong contender in your reviewing process.
I look forward to hearing from you.

Sincerely,
Hee-Young Kim
Head of Convention Team

[출처] IAEM(1999: 98)–Model Letters: A Guide for Effective Business Communication

Notes

on behalf of~ ~를 대신하여, ~를 대표하여
are noted for ~로 알려져 있다
proposal 제안서
alteration 변경사항
make every effort to ~하기 위해 모든 노력을 기울이다

2. 국제회의 유치를 위하여 PCO가 협회에 보내는 서한이다.

PCO name (sender)
address
date

name (receiver)
address

Dear Mr.

It is our pleasure to present for the consideration of the ABC Association, a detailed proposal of the services that PCO will provide for your 2017 Annual Meeting in Seoul, Korea.
This proposal is divided into three sections:
1. Introduction of PCO
2. Specific service we propose to provide
3. Advantages to ABC Association in using our services

When you have had a chance to look over the enclosed, we would very much appreciate the opportunity to discuss these arrangements with you and sincerely hope that you will choose PCO to coordinate arrangements for this important meeting.
I hope to set up an appointment at your convenience to discuss this with you.

Sincerely yours,
name
Sales Manager
PCO

Enclosure: 1. Introduction of PCO
2. Specific services we propose to provide
3. Advantages to ABC Association in using our service

[출처] 국제회의영어, 한광종

Notes

proposal 제안서
enclosed 동봉된(첨부된) 서류
at your convenience 당신이 편하신 시간에

1. Introduction Of PCO

PCO has been in operation for over 3 years, successfully specializing in the operation of conventions and exhibitions. Our staff of 5 employees are specially trained in coordinating arrangements for conventions and exhibitions.

2. Specific Service We Propose To Provide

Control of air reservations

We will reserve enough seats on the most convenient flight from all over the world to Korea on June 15, with return on June 21, to accommodate your members attending the meeting. We will also arrange return flights and ground arrangements for an optional post-meeting tour around Seoul.
The most convenient flights between Tokyo and Seoul, flights between Los

Angeles and Seoul are often filled far in advance, and thus by blocking space, we will assure your members of seats on the choice flight, even after the flight may be sold out to the general public.

Savings on air fares

By controlling the air seats for your members, we will be in a position to offer the maximum benefits on air travel, either based on a group fare, or on individual low fares.

Free tickets

By having all your members book their air reservations through our office, we will be able to coordinate the reservations and thus assure your Association the maximum benefits in the way of free tickets, so that you may use them to offset your costs of travel for staff or guest speakers.

Control of hotel reservations

By blocking sufficient hotel rooms in advance, we can assure your members appropriate accommodations with the best possible "group" rate and we can assure the Association of the maximum possible benefit in terms of complimentary hotel rooms.

Service Assistance at the meeting

On the officially appointed day, we will have a representative at the airport to personally meet participants, provide the traditional greeting, and direct the members to transportation to take them to the hotel. Luggage will be specially tagged and thus will be transported to the hotel and delivered to each person's room.

During the entire period of your meeting, our representative will be available at the hotel to take care of ay services your members may need, such as reconfirming airline reservations, setting up optional pre- and post convention tours, making arrangement for rented cars, giving local information, etc.

Promotional brochure

We will work with you to develop a brochure for your meeting, to be distributed

to your members. It is suggested that the contents include a preliminary program, full details on air travel, hotel accommodations, pre-and post-convention tours, and general information on Korea.
Also, it should include details and prices for the optional post-convention tour to the neighbor places, if you decide to include this.
The brochure will also include a reservation form, which your members can complete and thus accomplish registration for the meeting and reservations for hotel, air travel, and optional arrangements.

3. Advantages To ABC Association In Using The Service Of PCO

Travel services
Members of ABC Association will receive complete service in arranging their transportation, hotel, and other reservations for the meeting. Our staff will be working for your Association and members in coordinating arrangements and handling all details for those attending.

Promotional material
We will work with you to provide a satisfactory brochure for the meeting. Since we have coordinated arrangements for many other conventions of this nature we can offer many suggestions for the most efficient and detailed type of promotion piece. Some samples of brochures on previous conventions we have handled are enclosed for your perusal.

Trip escort
If the total participation on the convention is 20 or more persons, we will be happy to send along a staff from PCO to ensure that all arrangements are satisfactory for the meeting.
In all probability, the staff will be familiar with every detail of the arrangements. In this case we would use one of the complimentary hotel rooms for the staff. PCO would absorb the salary and other expenses.

[출처] 국제회의영어, 한광종

Notes

exhibition 전시회
return flight 귀국 항공편
in advance 미리
complimentary room 무료객실
hotel accommodation 호텔숙박
in all probability 아마도, 십중팔구는

Vocabulary

Write the word that best completes each sentence.

interpretation, announcement, summary, papers, agenda

1. First Announcement: 5th International Symposium on Architectural Interchanges in Asia and Call for ______________.

2. The conference delegates were provided with simultaneous ______________.

3. An ______________ was posted on the bulletin board.

4. Can you tell me about the meeting in ______________?

5. Let's review the ______________ for the workshop.

Global Countries and Culture

Italy

Rome

로마는 기독교세계의 중심지로서 이러한 역사의 유산을 도시 전체에서 찾아볼 수 있다. 로마 가톨릭의 수장인 교황은 로마 중심부에 자리한 독립국가 바티칸에 여전히 살고 있고, 가톨릭의 가장 성스러운 성당인 '성 베드로 대성당'에는 세계 각지의 많은 여행자와 순례자가 찾는다.

In the year 300 you could be killed for being a Christian. In the year 400 you could be killed for not being a Christian. Church attendance boomed, and Emperor Constantine built the first great Christian church right here — San Giovanni in Laterano...St. John's.

It opened as a kind of "first Vatican." St. John's — which has been rebuilt over the ages — was the original home of the bishop of Rome, or "Pope." High atop the canopy over the altar, a box supposedly contains bits of the skulls of Saint Peter and Saint Paul. The church is filled with symbols of Christianity's triumph over pagan Rome: For instance, tradition says these gilded bronze columns once stood in pagan Rome's holiest temple. And what better doors for this first grand church than those which once hung in ancient Rome's Senate House.

The adjacent Holy Stairs are a major stop on Rome's pilgrimage trail. Many credit Emperor Constantine's mother, St. Helena, for her son's conversion. She brought home wagonloads of relics including these stairs — believed to be from the palace of Pontius Pilate. For 1700 years pilgrims — believing Jesus climbed these stairs on the day he was condemned — have scaled the Scala Santa on their knees.

The influence of ancient Rome is everywhere. Its noble ruins tell a tale of power, politics, and imperial egos; of pagan gods now forgotten; of public art on a grand scale; and of enduring engineering feats. It's a story of colossal achievement and monumental failure.

By the year 500, the over-expanded, corrupt, and exhausted Roman Empire had fallen. But the grandeur of the Roman Empire lived on in the Roman Church. Over time, Trajan's column was capped with a Christian saint, the Pantheon became a church, Emperor Hadrian's mausoleum became the Pope's fortress, and the tomb of the Apostle Peter, a man the Romans executed, was crowned by the grandest building in the city — St. Peter's Basilica.

[출처] https://www.ricksteves.com

컨벤션기획사 영어시험문제

1. **다음의 (　　)에 알맞은 표현은?**

> The Host Committee will be glad to examine papers from all who are interested in submitting them. Ideally, these papers should not exceed five double-spaced typed pages (　　), should not use notes, should treat subjects of contemporary significance, and should be interesting and readable. If accepted presented papers will appear in the Conference Proceedings.

(A) at length　　(B) for a length of time

(C) in length　　(D) of some length

[어휘] submission of paper(s) 발표논문 제출 / examination of paper(s) 발표논문 심사 / acceptance(≠ rejection) of paper(s) 논문 채택 / presentation of paper(s) 논문 발표

정답 I C

2. **예약된 고객의 항공기가 연착하여 다음날 도착했을 경우, 전일의 방값까지 지불하는 요금은?**

(A) No-Show Rate　　(B) Midnight Charge

(C) Hold Room Charge　　(D) Cancellation Charge

[어휘] Hold room charge

고객이 예약하고, 아직 도착하지 않은 경우로서, 고객이 객실을 이용하지 않고 다른 곳에서 숙박했더라도 예약에 따라 지불해야 하는 객실요금을 의미한다.

정답 I B

3. 다음의 (　　)에 알맞은 표현은?

Thank you for the reminder about the 15th ABC Event!
I think it would be best if you flew in on Tuesday, May 12 and we hold the event on Wednesday. If we begin at 10:00, I'm sure we'll be finished by 4:30. Please (　　) so that I can arrange for someone to pick you up at the airport. I will book a room for you at the Hillside, as usual.

(A) conform your arrival details
(B) conform your departure details
(C) confirm your departure details
(D) confirm your arrival details

[어휘] conform 순응하다, 따르다

정답 I D

Exercise

국제경영학회 컨퍼런스 유치를 위하여 컨벤션센터를 홍보하는 편지를, 국내 및 해외 주요대학에 보내려고 합니다. 업무용 영문편지의 구성요소, 즉 편지 머릿부분(Letter Head), 날짜선(Date), 속지주소(Inside Address), 인사말(Salutation), 본문(Message), 마무리 인사(Closing), 그리고 서명자의 이름(Name) 등을 순서대로 배열해서 작성해 볼까요?

Hotel convention English

호텔컨벤션영어

UNIT 10

For Convention(II)

Hotel
convention
English

호텔컨벤션영어

Presentation

1.

Korea Convention Center의 시설담당자가 이 센터를 견학하러 온 방문객들에게 센터의 여러 활동을 서너 개의 부분으로 나누어 간략하게 설명하는 본론 부분의 발표다. 발표 내용을 연결해나가는데 적절한 연결구를 체크하면서 다음의 발표사례를 살펴보자.

Let's start with the history. Now don't worry! I'm not going to give you a history lesson, just a few key dates. The Korea Convention Center started out as a private limited.... So we've had a pretty eventful 20 years or so. Anyway, I'll leave the history there. If you're interested, you'll find more about KCC in this pretty brochure. You should find it amongst all the other pamphlets that PR people love to give out. So, let's turn now to a brief overview of our main markets. If you look at this chart, you'll see our slice of the pie, which in the European....

By the way, you may have seen the story in the news today about our main competitor, ABC Center. It seems they're going to bring out a new service product which could seriously infringe the copyright....

So, we'll have to wait and see how the market reacts. Anyway, let me get back to what I was saying about the new markets for KCC. I think it would be safe to say that....

Nobody really knows what the next century will bring. One thing that is certain is that you need people who can adapt quickly. And that brings me to the final part of this short introduction to KCC, and that is to talk about our people. As I said, they are our most important asset. We've even sponsored the staff for their overseas training. So, before I go on, are there any questions about our personnel policy?

[출처] 컨벤션영어, YoungJin.com

Notes

give out 배포하다
overview 개관, 개요
So, let's turn now to a brief overview of ~ 이제 ~에 대한 간략한 개요로 넘어가 보지요. (또 다른 화제를 시작하려고 할 때 사용하는 표현임)
competitor 경쟁자
infringe 침해하다, 침식하다
Anyway, let's get back to what I was saying about... 어쨌든 제가 드리려던 말씀내용으로 되돌아가 보지요. (설명이 조금 빗나가서 발표자가 본 내용으로 돌아가려고 할 때 쓸 수 있는 유용한 표현임)
adapt 적응하다
And that brings me to the final part of this short introduction to ~ 그렇게 해서 ~에 대한 간략한 설명의 마지막 부분이 이어지게 됩니다. (한 부분의 내용을 마무리 짓고 한때 유용한 표현임)

【단락연결】

Sequencing / Ordering(순서 열거하기)
firstly...secondly...thirdly...
then...next...finally / lastly...
Let's start with
Let's move/go on to...
Now we come to...
That brings us to...
Let's leave that...
That covers...
Let's get back to...

Comparing(비교)
Similarly
In the same say

Contradicting(모순)
In fact
Actually
Summarizing
To sum up
In brief
In short

Digressing(이탈)
By the way
In passing

Giving examples(예문)
for example
for instance
such as

Giving reasons / causes(이유)	Concluding(결론)	Generalizing(일반화)
Therefore	In conclusion	Usually
So	To conclude	Generally
As a result		As a rule
That's why	**Highlighting(강조)**	
	In particular	
Contrasting(대조)	Especially	
but		
however		

2.

발표내용을 마무리하는 적절한 표현은?

A.

Let me summarize the main issues as I see them. Firstly... Secondly... And thirdly... Hopefully this will help us to agree on a clear way forward. Are there any questions you'd like to ask?

Notes

summarize 요약하다

B.

Well, thank you for listening. That brings me to the end of this presentation. Before I leave you to get on with your work, I'd just like to say how glad we are to have you with us, and I wish you a very successful and happy time here at ICEM. Thank you.

Notes

get on with 시작하다, 착수하다

have you with us 우리와 함께 하다

C.

So, before I stop, let me just run over the key benefits. Firstly, flexibility: it'll work anywhere. We've tested it extensively and the results are excellent. Secondly, price: as you've seen, it's going to be highly competitive. And lastly, innovation: this is really a breakthrough in the field. Now, I'm sure you've got lots of questions, so fire away.

Notes

extensively 폭넓게

breakthrough 탈출구, 문제해결책

fire away 사격을 하다, 퍼붓다

D.

So, ladies and gentlemen, that completes my brief introduction. KCC is a fascinating property, and hopefully you'll get to know us better as you go around the facility. So let me hand you over to Mr. Jeong-Ryol Park, who's going to show you around.

Notes

get to ~하게 되다

hand over ~에게 넘기다

E.

That brings me to the end of my presentation. I realize that many of you already had some knowledge about our company. As you can see, we've got an impressive display of our products here. Why don't you come to our booth and get some hands-on experience?

Notes

impressive display 멋진 진열
hands-on 직접적인

3.

발표자가 자신을 소개하고 발표할 내용을 알려주는데 필요한 영어 표현을 정리해 보자.

A. Greeting, name, position

- Good morning, My name's (...) I'm the new Finance Manager.
- Ladies and gentlemen. It's an honour to have the opportunity to address such a distinguished audience.
- Good morning. Let me start by saying just a few words about my own background. I started out in ...
- Welcome to Standard Electronics. I know I've met some of you, but just for the benefit of those I haven't, my name's (...).

B. Title / Subject

- I'd like to talk (to you) today about ...
- I'm going to present the recent ...

  explain our position on ...

  brief you on ...

  inform you about ...

  describe ...

- The subject of my talk

    focus presentation(adacemic)

    topic speech(usually to public audience)

C. Purpose / Objective

- We are here today to decide ...

    agree...

    learn about...

- The purpose of this talk is to update you on...

    put you in the picture about...

    give you the background to...

- This tale is designed to act as a springboard for discussion.

    start the ball rolling.

D. Length

- I shall only take (...) minute of your time.
- I plan to be brief.
- This should only last (...) minutes.

E. Outline / Main parts

- I've divided my presentation into four parts / sections. They are ...
- The subject can be looked at under the following headings...
- We can break this area down into the following fields.

    Firstly / first of all ...

    Secondly / then/next ...

    Thirdly / and then we come to ...

    Finally / lastly / last of all ...

F. Questions

- I'd be glad to answer any questions at the end of my talk. If you have any questions, please feel free to interrupt.
- Please interrupt me if there is something which needs clarifying. Otherwise, there'll be time for discussion at the end.

G. Reference to the audience

- I can see many of you are ...
- I know you're all travelled a long way.
- You all look as though

[출처] Comfort(1996:14) Effective Presentations

Writing Tips

1. 등록안내편지 – 등록에 관해 참가자들에게 알리는 편지

December 10, 2002

Dear AAOJ Dazzling Diamonds Show Attendee:

Thank you for pre-registering for the 2003 Dazzling Diamonds Tradeshow taking place on February 12-14 in Uptown, Arizona at the Majestic County Convention Center. The enclosed confirmation packet contains your badges along with hotel information, exhibitor list, event and scheduling information. Please review the badges carefully, and if you have any questions, call the AAOJ office at (800)888-8888.

Please bring your badges with you to the show. If needed, replacement badges will be available for $15 each at the registration area in the lobby of the Majestic County Convention Center. Badge holders and show directories will be available free of charge at the show registration area.

If you haven't already done so make your hotel reservation immediately to ensure availability. You can reach Travel Technicians at (800)333-3333 to make your reservation.

We appreciate your support of the Dazzling Diamonds Tradeshow and look forward to seeing you in Uptown.

Sincerely,
American Association of Jewelers

Reid Maitland
Executive Director

[출처] IAEM(1999: 69)–Model Letters: A Guide for Effective Business Communication

Notes

pre-registering for ~를 사전 등록하기
take place 개최되다
directory 참가자 명부
free of charge 무료로

2. 등록안내 – 현장등록안내

Registration Procedures
Conferences, Event and Exhibit Hall -- On-Site Registration

Badges Available: Conference
Conference / Tutorial
Exhibits Only
Exhibitor
Speaker
Press
For Attendee Registration.

Paid Attendees
- Complete an on-site registration form(4-part NCR form) located at sign-in counters.
- Take completed form together with payment to Cashier.
- Take yellow and pink copies of registration form to Typist.
- Typist gives attendee their receipt (pink copy of registration form) and directs attendee to printer station to pick up a badge.

Complimentary Attendees
- Show a Pass and complete the on-site registration form.
- Go directly to Self-Registration. OR proceed directly to Typist.
- After Typist enters registration date, proceed to printer station to pick up a badge.

[출처] IAEM(1999:60)

Notes

paid attendee(s) 등록비를 낸 참가자(들)
sign-in counter 접수대
printer station 프린터기가 있는 곳
complementary attendee(s) 무료 참가자(들)
self-registration 직접 컴퓨터에 입력하여 등록하기

Vocabulary

Write the word that best completes each sentence.

convention, aircraft, inquiry, registration, reminder

1. Will you fill out this ________________ form?

2. Another name for an airplane is ________________.

3. Thank you for your ________________ about our new products.

4. All the hotels are full because of the ________________.

5. The flight attendant sometimes gives passengers a ________________ to turn off electronic equipment.

Global Countries and Culture

Italy
The best of Venice

한때 유럽의 최고 권력의 도시이고 쾌락의 도시이던 베니스를, 주 도로인 운하를 따라서 여행한다. 가면무도회의 멋진 마스크들을 구경하고 도나텔로와 벨리니 같은 르네상스시대 거장들의 예술작품을 감상하고 달빛 아래 곤돌라를 타고 낭만에 젖어본다.

Throughout Europe, rich and poor enjoyed a burst of pre-Lenten fun during the annual festival called Carnavale. For the festival of Venice, Carnavale, these masks are a key part - giving everyone anonymity. And today, local artisans keep shoppers well supplied with these icons of Venice.

Along with many colorful masks, shoppers target Venetian glass. The glass industry has long been important in Venice - and it still is for tourists. You can adorn your palazzo with a brilliant chandelier of Venetian glass…or pick up a vase, or some beads.

In Venice, I sleep in the old center - ideally in a 400-year-old hotel, waking to the clang of church bells. Family-run, centuries old, friendly, characteristic and well-located, Pensione Gueratto is the kind of place I'd like to recommend and it's my home in Venice - just around the corner from the Rialto Bridge.

Art lovers can spend their days touring Venice's top-notch art galleries. But my favorite art experience in Venice? The Franciscan "Church of the Friars" and the art that decorates it. It features the work of three great Renaissance masters: Donatello, Bellini, and Titian - each showing worshippers the glory of God in human terms. Donatello's wood carving of St. John the Baptist, the prophet of the desert. Bellini's beautiful paintings of Madonna and Saints. Finally, Titian's Assumption, glowing red and gold like a stained glass window.

And for open-air art, you need only to look at the canals. Venice's sleek and graceful gondolas are a symbol of the city. From the start, boats were the way to get around among the island communities of the lagoon.

Well, today, a gondola ride is a traditional must for romantics. Gondolas are moored everywhere. Just settle on a price and hop in. The 40-minute rides are expensive but you can divide the cost by up to six people. Since you might get a fun tour or impromptu conversation with your gondolier, talk with several and choose the one you enjoy the most.

[출처] https://www.ricksteves.com

컨벤션기획사 영어시험문제

1. 다음 편지에 대한 내용으로 맞는 것은?

Dear Gentlemen and Ladies:

The enclosed check for $312.68 is in payment of invoice no. 10463.
Please credit my account(no. 663-711-M).

Yours truly,

(A) 이 편지에 $312,68이 동봉되어 있다.

(B) 동봉한 통장계좌번호는 10463이다.

(C) 지불청구로 $312.68을 요구하는 편지다.

(D) 송금요청에 대해 외상거래를 부탁하고 있다.

[어휘] invoice 청구서, 대금청구서

정답 I A

2. 다음 글의 요지를 가장 잘 나타낸 것은?

The goal of convention and visitor bureaus is to make planning and implementing your conventions and meetings less time-consuming, less stressful and more streamlined. Bureaus - both across the nation and around the world - are ready to assist you in every detail of planning your event. And most of their services are free. Whether you represent a billion-dollar corporation, a small family business, or any size association just one call or e-mail connects you with a team of professionals who are experts on their respective destinations.

(A) Convention bureaus make the planning of meetings more efficient.

(B) Convention bureaus make lots of money.

(C) Convention bureaus want to work only with big corporation.

(D) Convention bureaus employ many professionals.

[어휘] implement 이행하다 / respective destination 해당 목적지, 각각의 목적지 정답 I A

3. **다음 계약서 서식 영문표현 중 잘못된 것은?**

> The performance of this agreement by either party(①) is subject to acts of law(②), government regulation, disaster, strikes, civil disorder, curtailment of transportation facilities(③), or other emergency making it advisable, illegal or impossible to provide the facilities or to hold(④) the meeting convention.

(A) ① (B) ② (C) ③ (D) ④

[어휘] transportation facility 교통편 시설 / illegal 비합법적인 정답 I B

4. **다음 중 아래 편지에 동봉된 것은?**

> Dear Ms. Kim
>
> Enclosed is the form for paying your business license tax for 2011. Please complete the form and return it with payment no later than February 1, 2012. Make checks payable to Treasurer.
>
> Sincerely,
>
> John White
> Commissioner

(A) a check (B) a business license

(C) a form (D) a picture

[어휘] commissioner 위원, 이사 / treasurer 회계 / enclosed is ~을 동봉한다 정답 I C

Exercise

다음 내용을 담고 있는 행사의 참가자 등록양식을 영어로 작성해 볼까요?

1. 회의명 : FIPP Seoul 2018(기간 : 2018년 4월 16~18일)
2. 참가자 : 이름, 성별, 소속기관, 부서명, 직책, 연락처
3. 동반자 : 동반자 수, 성별, 이름, 개인적 요청사항
4. 참가자 등록비
   - 조기 사전등록(US $750) / 사전등록(US $900) / 현장등록(US $1,000)
   - 모든 세션, 리셉션, 만찬, 환송만찬, 점심 등 비용 포함
5. 동반자 등록비
   - 1인당 US $500×인원수
   - 리셉션, 환송만찬, 동반자 프로그램 비용 포함
6. 관광프로그램 신청(3~4종의 코스, 비용, 날짜 표기)
   - 고궁관광은 27달러로, 4월 15일 09:00~12:00
   - 야간 쇼핑관광은 55달러로, 4월 17일 19:00~22:30
   - 판문점 관광은 60달러로, 4월 20일 09:00~17:00
   - 세계문화유산관광은 48달러로, 4월 16일 09:00~17:00
7. 지불방법 : (은행구좌나 신용카드로)

UNIT 11

For Convention(III)

Hotel
convention
English

호텔컨벤션영어

Questions & Answers

1.

질의응답을 어떻게 할까요?

A.

1. A: May I ask a question?

   B: Please, do.
2. A: Do you mind telling me where you got those figures?

   B: Well, actually, it's confidential.
3. A: Don't you think we need to take a break?

   B: That's a good idea.
4. A: Could I ask you when you're going to leave?

   B: Any moment.

Notes

confidential 대외비의
take a break 잠깐 쉬다
any moment 곧

B.

1. A: Excuse me, could I interrupt?

   B: Of course.

   A: I'd like to ask you about next year's promotion campaign.

   B: Sure, what exactly would you like to know?

A: Well, could you tell me at this stage whether you have fixed a budget?

B: We've got a meeting next week to decide. I'll let you know straight away, if that's OK.

A: Sure, that'll be fine.

2. A: So, that brings me to the end of my presentation. I'd be glad to answer any question.

B: I was interested to hear what you had to say about our on-line registration software. Do you think it has any real future?

A: Certainly I do. However, we can't expect the same level of revenues we've generated over the last ten years. Wouldn't you agree?

B: I suppose so. It worries me that we don't have any backup equipment. Doesn't it worry you, too?

A: Well, that's difficult to say. It's true we haven't come up with a backup for the B43. On the other hand, as I pointed out, we have new softwares for upgrading our homepage.

C: On that subject. I'd like to ask you about the C11. Can you tell us how much longer before it's ready for use?

A: That's not really my field. Dr. Gillae Kim should be able to give you an idea about that.

C: Right, I'll talk to him after the meeting.

D: So-yeon, could I ask you about the delays on our new A15?

A: Please, go ahead.

D: Well, as you know, we've put together a fairly large-scale advertising campaign. Was all the space booked for the October trade show?

A: Don't worry. We'll be ready for the date. There are one or two technical problems, but they won't delay us much longer.

D: That's good to hear.

[출처] 컨벤션영어, YoungJin.com

Notes

interrupt 중단하다, 방해하다
have fixed a budget 예산을 확정했다
That brings me to the end of my presentation 발표를 마치겠다
revenue 수입
we've generated 창출해 왔다
It worries me that 저는 이런 걱정이 든다
point out 지적하다
large-scale 대규모의
was booked for ~를 위해 예약했다

2.

질의응답 – 영어표현 요약

A. Direct question

Do you have any plans for another banquet?

Where do you plan to staff them?

B. Polite question and answers

QUESTIONS

Do you mind if I ask you

Would you mind telling me if / where...

Could / Can you tell me what / where / etc...

I'm interested to know about / I'd like to know

ANSWERS

Go ahead / Please do / Certainly

That's a good question

That's interesting.

C. Statement question and answers

QUESTIONS

All the space was booked for the October Eradeshow...?

It worries me that we don't have any backup equipment. Doesn't it worry you too?

ANSWERS

1. A: It's going to be late, isn't it?
   B: I'm afraid so.
   A: You've got problems with the logistics?
   B: Yes, a few.
   A: The suppliers have done their job.
   B: Is that right?
   A: Yes, as far as I know.
2. A: We haven't won the contract, have we?
   B: No, it doesn't look like it.
   A: We aren't going to make it on time, are we?
   B: I'm afraid not.
   A: The company's going to close, isn't it?
   B: Well, actually, I've just heard the company is employing more staff.

D. Clarifying a question

If I understand you correctly, you are saying / asking...

I didn't quite catch that

Could you go over that again?

I'm not sure what you're getting at.

E. Avoiding giving and answer

Perhaps we could deal with that later.

Can we talk about that on another occasion?

I'm afraid that's not my field.

I don't have the figures with me.

That's interesting, but I'd prefer not to answer that today.

F. Checking the questioner is satisfied.

Does that answer your question?

Is that clear?

May we go on?

[출처] Comfort(1996:47)

Notes

focus on ~에 초점을 맞추다
work 작동하다, 운영되어 가다
strategy 전략
turnover 총매출액
front 측면, 현장
recruit 신입사원을 모집하다
the sort of influence he can have on ~에 미칠 수 있는 일종의 영향력
promote 증진시키다

Writing Tips

1. 문의에 대한 답장

Dear Mr. X:

Thank you for your request for information about the ABC Conference Center. One of Seoul's newest facilities, we are a full-service meeting center just a few minutes from City Hall.

The enclosed brochure describes our special features, including small and medium-size meeting rooms and professional staff.

If you drop by ABC Conference Center any time between 7 a.m. and 10 p.m., we would be delighted to give you a personal tour of the Center.

Cordially yours,

[출처] Geffner(1995: 39), How to Write Better Business Letter

Notes

feature 특성
drop by 잠깐 들리다
be delighted to 기꺼이 ~하다
tour 안내

2. 확인편지 – 예약 확인편지

The Barclay
5500 south 96th Street, Omaha, Nebraska 68127
August, 10, 2008

Mr. Yegor Volsky
2233 Connecticut Avenue, N.W.
Washington, D.C. 2008

Dear Mr. Volsky

This letter will confirm your reservation for a single room with bath for August 24-27. Your room will be available after 2 p.m. on the 24th.

Since you will be arriving in Omaha by plane, you may want to take advantage of the Barclay's Shuttle. Our limousine departs from the domestic terminal every hour, and the service is free for guests of the hotel.

Cordially yours,

[출처] Geffner(1995: 34)

Notes

confirm 확인하다
take advantage of 이용하다
domestic terminal 국내선 터미널

3. 거절의 편지

October 8, 2003

Mr. Derek Jourdan
Jourdan Jems
3220 Ruby Ridge Road
Amber, TX 75222

Dear Derek:

Thank you for your recent inquiry about space availability for your upcoming event. Unfortunately, we do not have the space to accommodate your group during the time frame requested. If there is any possibility of revising your scheduled dates, please let us now, as we would be happy to accommodate your organization at any other time.

If I may be of further assistance in helping you find other facilities, please do not hesitate to contact me.

Thank you for your initial interest. We wish you success and hope that we will have an opportunity to extend our hospitality to you sometime in the future.

Sincerely,

PURPLE SAGE RESORT & SPA

Zane Lamour
Sales Manager

[출처] IAEM(1999: 55)

Notes

inquiry 문의
the time frame 그 기간대
revising 변경하기
extend 전달하다

Vocabulary

Write the word that best completes each sentence.

speaker, attendees, expiration date, carry-on luggage, boarding pass

1. Each traveler is allowed two pieces of ________________.

2. A ________________ is the slip of paper you hand over before getting on the airplane.

3. Passports are valid for a limited time and they always have an ________________.

4. He has consumed the eight minutes allowed per ________________.

5. Send a cancel notification to ________________.

Global Countries and Culture

Scandinavia
Helsinki and Tallinn: Baltic Sisters

핀란드 사람들이 즐기는 사우나를 둘러본 후, 헬싱키에서 두 시간 배를 타고 에스토니아로 가서 세계를 놀라게 한 인간띠 혁명의 현장을 찾아본다. 남쪽에 있는 리투아니아에서부터 시작하여 라트비아를 거쳐 에스토니아에 이르는 620km의 도로에, 기나긴 인간사슬을 만들어 수많은 사람들이 손에 손을 잡고 하루 종일 노래를 불렀고, 전 세계의 이목이 여기에 집중되었으며, 마침내 소련은 그들의 독립을 허용하기에 이른다.

Helsinki is set in a natural wonderland. And hopping a boat tour for a 90-minute cruise makes that very clear. The several hundred islands of its archipelago provide a delightful playground. Many have family cabins there, and a standard feature is a free-standing sauna(...)

Nearby is the stage from where the people of Estonia gathered to demand their independence. The Song Festival Grounds, which hosts massive choral festivals, is a uniquely Estonian institution. This is a national monument because of the stirring role it played in Estonia's fight for independence.

With only a million people, lodged between Russia and Germany, and without a strong military, Estonians asserted themselves with song. They say being together and singing together was their power.

Rick: 300,000 Estonians gathering here to sing together…

Mati: Yeah, one day in 1988, one third of the Estonian nation gathered here to sing. To sing about the freedom, about the independence, to show to the rest of the world and especially to the Soviet side that we are tired to be one part of the Soviet system. And, as we can see now, almost 20 years later, that it was successful.

Tallinn's Museum of the Occupation rounds out the story. Suitcases are a reminder of people who fled the country leaving everything behind. Displays show how Russians managed to keep the Estonians in line. Surveillance was a part of daily life. Prison doors evoke the countless lives lost in detention and deportation. And the communist leaders who once lorded over the Estonian people are now in the basement guarding the toilets.

With freedom, Tallinn has revealed its unique charm with its medieval Old Town witnessing the emergence of a new prosperity.

[출처] https://www.ricksteves.com

컨벤션기획사 영어시험문제

1. **아래의 글은 어떤 행사를 위한 초대문인가?**

> On behalf of the organization committee, I am greatly honored to invite professionals in the field of cardiac and pulmonary vascular anesthetists to join this international congress in Seoul, Korea. The occasion will be a lively forum for exchanging important research findings and practical knowledge.

(A) Government symposium
(B) Meeting for NGOs
(C) Domestic convention
(D) Medical conference

[어휘] pulmonary 폐의 / vascular 혈관의 / anesthetist 마취의

정답 I D

2. **다음 중 연사에게 제공되지 않는 사항은?**

> As a speaker at the symposium, you will be provided with a round trip air ticket in business class, lodging expenses at the venue hotel (excluding the use of telephone and mini bar), and complimentary registration.

(A) Lodging house
(B) Hotel accommodation
(C) Flight
(D) Exemption from registration

[어휘] venue 회의 개최장소 / complimentary breakfast 조식 무료제공

정답 I A

3. 다음 글의 밑줄 친 약자의 뜻은?

Please check and return the R.S.V.P. slip to the hospitality desk. Hotel Emerald Lobby, where you'll be given tickets for the program you want to attend.

(A) 회신 (B) 코냑

(C) 중요인사 (D) 등록서류

[어휘] R.S.V.P. Répondez S'il Vous Plaît. 정답 I A

4. 다음 편지의 내용에 관한 설명으로 옳은 것은?

Dear Mr. Volsky:

This letter confirms your reservation for a single room with bath for August 24-27. Your room will be available after 2 p.m. on the 24th. Since you will be arriving in Omaha by plane, you may want to take advantage of the Barclay's shuttle. Our limousine departs from the domestic terminal every hour on the half hour, and the service is free for guests of the hotel.

(A) The Barclay is the hotel where Mr. Volsky will stay.

(B) Mr. Volsky is the limousine airport bus driver.

(C) The shuttle bus runs every 30 minutes between Omaha and Barclay.

(D) Mr. Volsy is flying into Omaha from abroad to visit the Barclay.

[어휘] domestic terminal 국내선터미널 정답 I A

Exercise

컨벤션기획사 2급 시험문제에 제출되었던 '연사안내 지침자료' 문제를 풀어볼까요?

Q. 다음 내용을 담고 있는 연사안내 지침자료를 영어로 작성하시오.

1. 행사주최 본부인 The International Federation of the Periodical Press(FIPP)가 연사들에게 연설수락에 대한 감사
2. 연설문 원고를 E-mail로 요청(마감일은 늦어도 행사시작 2주 전)
3. 연사 소개내용(50~100단어) 및 사진(인쇄 및 웹사이트용)을 E-mail로 요청
4. 필요한 기자재 요청
5. 보낼 곳 : Mr. Key C. Min / Korea Convention Service
6. 발표당일날 : 미리 Speaker's Room에서 연습 요청
7. 의장 / 사회자 주의사항 : 회의진행 시 시간 엄수, 각 발표자 소개, 예상질문 준비, 세션 종료 후 감사, 공지사항 안내, 다음 세션 안내

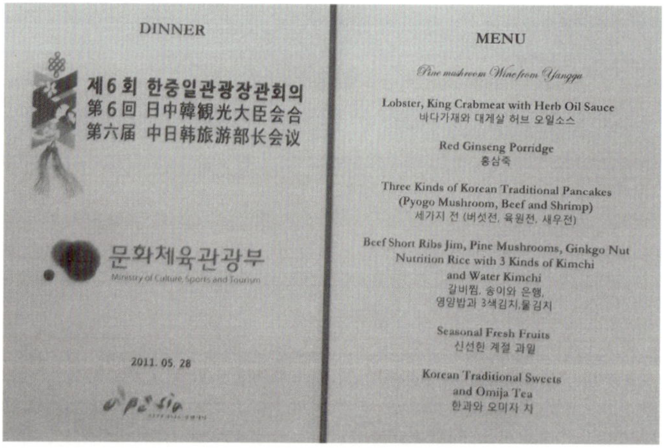

UNIT 12

For Convention(IV)

Hotel
convention
English

호텔컨벤션영어

개회사

국제회의의 개회사와 폐회사, 그리고 축사를 순서대로 살펴보자. 여기서는 먼저 Opening Address의 한 사례(2017 고령화 국제심포지엄)를 소개한다.

I. Opening Remarks

Honored Guests and Distinguished Participants,
I am OOO, Commissioner of Statistics Korea. It is my great pleasure to welcome all of you to the Global Symposium on Ageing co-hosted by Statistics Korea and the United Nations Population Fund.

I would like to express my special thanks to the Executive Director of the UNFPA, OOO and the experts from over 30 countries around the world, for taking the time out of their busy schedules to visit Korea.

This year marks fifteen years since the United Nations and representatives of member states and international organizations adopted of the Madrid International Plan of Action on Ageing (MIPAA) in 2002 and called for concerted action.

The aim of the MIPAA is to promote a healthy society for all age groups, and to ensure the happiness of a rapidly increasing older generation so that we leave no one behind. In commemoration of the fifteenth year since the MIPAA, I would like to recognize the significance of the cooperation of Statistics Korea and the UNFPA to hold this Global Symposium on Ageing to review the international implementation of the MIPAA and unfold new policy horizons in the upcoming decades.

II. Meaning of Symposium

Distinguished participants,
Ever since the late twentieth century, demographic change is gaining momentum not only in developed, but also in developing countries, as a world phenomenon. Population ageing, when the birth rate is unprecedentedly low and life expectancy is steadily heading toward 100 years, is directly affecting all sectors of our society.

When swept up unprepared, class polarization widens and individuals' quality of life deteriorates. In Korea, for example, 13.8% of the total population is made up of older persons aged 65 years and over. As of 2016, one out of three households with older persons is a single-person household. Half of the people in these single older person households are in their seventies. More than 25% of them are in their eighties.

Traditionally, older persons in Korea were supported by their children or relatives. Now 42% of older persons have to make their own living. 30.7% of older persons are currently employed. The older population will increase more dramatically. This is a phenomenon which is not limited to one or two societies. Now is the time for the international society to find a way forward to secure the quality of life for everyone of all ages. If we could overcome the problems associated with population ageing and find a way to secure the quality of older person's lives, population ageing will not be a disaster but a new opportunity for better social development.

This Symposium consists of three sessions in accordance with the three pillars of the MIPAA. They are ① Older persons and development ② Advancing health and well-being into old age and ③ Ensuring an enabling and supportive environment. Experts in each session will share their research, presentations, and discussions focusing on the three pillars. I believe this academic dedication will contribute to the successful monitoring of the policy issues listed in the MIPAA.

III. Contribution of Statistics Korea

Distinguished participants,
Statistics Korea has taken an active role in improving population statistics around the world and increasing the capacity for demographic data analysis. We are holding an annual Summer Seminar on Population to strengthen population statistics and data analysis capacities in developing countries. Last autumn, we co-organized an expert group meeting on civil registration and vital statistics with the United Nations Population Division.

Statistics Korea is also serving as the secretariat of the Association of National Census and Statistics Directors of America, Asia and Pacific (ANCSDAAP) and has organized a series of Population Census Conferences at intervals of two years for heads of national census and statistical offices as well as intranational organizations and academia.

I assure you that Statistics Korea will continue to be a responsible member of the international community for supporting and strengthening the capacities of the community and itself to address problems of population ageing and analyze the phenomena to turn the table for new opportunities and development.

IV. Closing Remarks

Ladies and Gentlemen,
The autumn season of Korea has long been called "the season of plump horses and high skies". It means that everything is rich in autumn and the weather is very pleasant. I hope you enjoy the beautiful autumn sky in Korea. I wish you success at this symposium and for a society ensuring everyone's happiness.

Lastly, I would like to acknowledge the staff members of the UNFPA, Statistics Korea, and the APPI for all the effort and time they put into this seminar. Thank you very much for your attention.

2017 고령화 국제심포지엄

개 회 사

2017. 10.

통계청장

I. 인사말씀

존경하는 내·외 귀빈 여러분,
통계청장 OOO입니다. 통계청과 유엔인구기금(UNFPA)이 공동으로 주최하는 “2017 고령화 국제심포지엄”에 참석하신 모든 분들을 진심으로 환영합니다. 특히, 바쁘신 일정에도 불구하고 한국을 찾아주신 유엔인구기금(UNFPA) OOO 총재님, 발표와 토론에 참여하시는 30여개국, 90여명의 세계적인 전문가 여러분들께도 감사의 말씀을 드립니다. 올해는 국제연합에서 국제기구, 각국의 대표들과 함께 2002년에 “마드리드 국제고령화선언(MIPAA)”을 채택하고 각국에 권고한 지 15년이 되는 해입니다.

마드리드 국제고령화선언은 “모든 연령계층의 사회”를 창출하고, 급증하는 고령자들의 행복을 보장하는 “뒤 어지는 자가 없는” 사회를 목표로 하고 있습니다. 마드리드 국제고령화선언의 15년이 되는 해에 국제적인 이행 상황 재점검과, 앞으로의 새로운 정책 방향 도출을 위해 한국통계청이 유엔인구기금과 공조하여 “2017 고령화 국제심포지엄”을 개최하게 된 것은 매우 의미 있다고 할 것입니다.

II. 심포지엄 개최의 의의

내·외 귀빈 여러분,
20세기 후반부터 점점 빨라지는 인구변동은 선진국만의 문제가 아니라 개발도상국을 포함한 전 세계적인 현상입니다. 출산율이 유례없이 낮아지고, 100세 시대를 바라보는 고령화는 사회 각 분야에 직접적인 영향을 주고 있습니다. 특히, 준비할 시간도 없이 닥쳐오는 고령화와 고령인구의 급증은 계층 간의 격차를 키우고, 개인의 삶의 질을 떨어뜨리고 있습니다. 우리나라의 예를 들면, 현재 한국은 전체 인구 중 13.8%가 65세 이상 고령자입니다. 2016년 기준으로 보면 고령자만 있는 가구 셋 중 하나 꼴로 홀로 사는 것으로 나타났습니다. 더욱이 고령자 1인 가구의 절반이 70대이고, 80세 이상 가

구도 25%가 넘습니다.

우리나라의 과거 전통은 고령자는 자녀나 친지의 도움으로 생활을 꾸려가는 것입니다만, 지금은 이들의 42%가 스스로 생활비를 마련하고 있고, 실제 고령자의 30.7%가 취업활동을 하고 있습니다. 문제는 고령자 인구가 앞으로 더 빨리 증가한다는 것입니다. 우리 사회만의 현상이 아니므로 국제사회가 힘을 합하여 고령사회에서 모두의 삶의 질을 확보할 수 있는 길을 찾아야 할 때입니다. 많은 사람들이 우려하는 고령화 문제를 극복하고, 고령자 삶의 질을 보장할 수 있는 길을 찾는다면고 령화는 재앙이 아니라 새로운 사회발전을 위한 기회가 될 것입니다.

이번 심포지엄에서는 마드리드 국제고령화선언의 세 가지 필라(pillars)에 따라 ① 고령화와 발전문제 ② 고령자 건강과 복지증진 ③ 고령자 지원환경 구축으로 세션을 구성하였습니다. 각 세션에서의 세 가지 필라(pillars)에 대한 전문가들의 연구결과 발표와 토론은 앞으로 마드리드 국제고령화선언의 성공적 이행에 도움이 될 것으로 확신합니다.

III. 한국통계청의 기여

내 · 외 귀빈 여러분,
한국통계청은 세계 각국의 인구통계 개선과 인구자료 분석을 위한 역량증진을 위해 적극 노력하고 있습니다. 개발도상국의 인구통계와 인구분석 역량강화를 위하여 매년 인구서머세미나를 개최하고 있으며, 작년 가을에는 유엔인구처(UNPD)와 공동으로 인구등록과 인구동태 통계에 관한 전문가회의를 개최하였습니다.

또한 아메리카 · 아시아 · 태평양 지역 인구센서스 기관장협의회(ANCSDAAP) 사무국 기능을 수행하고 있으며, 2년마다 아태지역 국가대표들이 참여하는 인구센서스회의를 개최하여, 지역 내 인구센서스와 인구통계 발전에 기여하고 있습니다. 앞으로도, 한국 통계청은 국제사회가 급변하는 인구 고령화 현상을 정확하게 파악하고 분석하는 능력을 키워 새로운 발전의 기회를 만드는데 적극 동참할 것입니다.

Ⅳ. 맺음말

내 · 외귀빈 여러분,
예로부터 한국의 가을은 "천고마비의 계절"이라고 합니다. 가을 하늘이 맑고 가을에는 모든 것이 풍요롭다는 뜻입니다. 맑고 아름다운 한국의 가을을 마음껏 즐기시고, 모두가 행복한 고령사회를 위한 이번 심포지엄의 성공을 기원합니다.

끝으로, 고령화 국제심포지엄을 준비해 주신 유엔인구기금, 한국통계청과 아태인구연구원 관계자들의 노고에 대해 다시 한 번 감사의 말씀을 드립니다.
감사합니다.

Writing Tips

1. 초청장

저희 코엑스는 지난 한해 고객여러분의 협조에 감사드리고
아울러 전시컨벤션업계 여러분의 교류를 증진시키기 위해 아래와 같이
2002 전시컨벤션의 밤을 개최하오니 부디 참석하시어
자리를 빛내주시기 바랍니다.

– 아 래 –

2002. 12. 12(목) 오후 6시 00분
무역센터 코엑스 1층 그랜드 볼룸

코엑스 대표이사 안 재 학

참석여부: (02)6000-1082, 1084

We cordially invite you to attend the Convention & Exhibition Night 2002, where you will have the opportunity to meet a variety of professionals in the industry.

on DEC. 12, 2002 at 6:00p.m.
COEX, Grand Ballroom, 1st floor

An, Jae-Hak
President of COEX(Convention & Exhibition)

RSVP: (02)6000-1082, 1084

[출처] 컨벤션영어, 서승진·윤은주 공저

Notes

cordially 정중하게
professional 전문인

2. 초청장 – 공식연회

In honor of
His Excellency the Prime Minister of the State of Travel and Mrs.
Benjamin Netanyahu
The President of the Republic of Korea
and Mrs. Kim Dae-Jung
Request the pleasure of the company of

at a Dinner
On Wednesday, the twenty-fifth of February
at six-thirty p.m.
at Chong Wa Dae

Lounge Suite on
National Dress

귀하
동영부인
네탄야후 이스라엘 총리 내 · 외분을 위하여
다음과 같이 만찬을 가지고자 하오니 참석하여
주시기 바랍니다.

일시 : 1998년 0월 00일 (수) 오후 6시
장소 : 청와대 본관
복장 : 평복

대통령 김 대 중
이 희 호

[출처] 컨벤션영어, 서승진

Notes

in honor of ~를 기리기 위해
His Excellency ~각하
request the pleasure of the company of ~로의 참석에 대한 기쁨을 요청한다는 의미로서, 공식적인 참가요청 문구임

3. 초청장 - 개회식

On the occasion of
the FIPP Asia-Pacific Magazine Media Regional Conference 2002 in Seoul
Mr. O O O
Conference Chairman of the Organizing Committee of FIPP Seoul Conference 2002
requests the pleasure of your company
at the Opening Ceremony
on Wednesday, April 17, 2002 at 0900
at Harmony Ballroom (B1 Fl.), Coex Inter-Continental Hotel

R.S.V.P. Tel: +82-2-552-8649

FIPP 아 · 태지역 잡지매체 서울대회 2002를 개최함에 있어 귀하를 모시고
다음과 같이 개회식을 갖고자 하오니 부디 참석하시어
자리를 빛내주시기 바랍니다.

일시 : 2002년 4월 17일(수) 오전 9시
장소 : 코엑스 인터컨티넨탈호텔 하모니볼룸 (지하 1층)

FIPP 서울대회 2002 조직위원회
대회조직위원장 O O O

참석여부회신 : FIPP 서울대회 2002 조직위원회 사무국
(Tel : 02-552-8649, Fax : 02-552-8325)

[출처] 컨벤션영어, 서승진

Vocabulary

Write the word that best completes each sentence.

declare, statement, honored, cordial welcome, pleasant stay

1. I'd like to extend a ________________ to you all gathered here to participate in the 5th World Congress of Scout.

2. I wish you a ________________ in the Republic of Korea and a safe return to your countries.

3. I now ________________ open the 60th session of the General Assembly.

4. I am ________________ to speak in this debate.

5. I thank the Prime Minister of Canada for the ________________ he has just made.

Global Countries and Culture

Scandinavia

Sweden: Stockholm

스톡홀름에 있는 노벨上박물관에는 1901년의 첫 회 수상자들의 얼굴을 비롯하여 현재까지의 노벨수상자들의 초상화가 전시되어 있고, 또한 이곳 시청홀에서는 매년 노벨상 시상식과 연회가 열린다.

Stockholm's Nobel Prize Museum tells the story of the world's most prestigious award. Stockholm-born Alfred Nobel was a prolific inventor with over 300 patents. His most famous invention? Dynamite.

Living in the late 1800s, Nobel was a man of his age. It was a time of great optimism, wild ideas, and grand projects. His dynamite enabled entire nations to blast their way into the modern age with canals, railroads, and tunnels. It made warfare much more destructive, and it also made Alfred Noble a very wealthy man.

Wanting to leave a legacy that celebrated and supported people with great ideas, he left his fortune to fund the Nobel Prize. Each year laureates are honored in the fields of physics, chemistry, medicine, literature, and perhaps most famously in peacemaking. Portraits of all the prizewinners since the first annual ceremony was held in 1901 hang from the ceiling — shuffling around the room like shirts at the dry cleaner's. And video clips let you ponder the contributions of so many great minds.

The annual Nobel Prize banquet is held just a short walk away, in Stockholm's City Hall. It's a stately mix of eight million red bricks and lots of Stockholm pride. While churches dominate cities in southern Europe, up here, in the Scandinavian capitals, city halls seem to be the most impressive buildings. They celebrate humanism...people working together for the good of their community. Built in 1923, Stockholm's City Hall is particularly enjoyable, and well worth its entertaining hour-long tour.

[출처] https://www.ricksteves.com

컨벤션기획사 영어시험문제

1. 다음의 (　　)에 각각 알맞은 표현은?

> (①) of the Opening Ceremony, the President of ABC requests the pleasure of your (②) at the Dinner on Thursday, October 12, 2017.

(A) In the occasion, Excellency　　(B) For the event, delegates

(C) On the occasion, participants　　(D) On the occasion, company

[어휘] delegates 대표 / company 참석(= presence, participation)

정답 I D

2. 다음 대화에서 A와 B의 관계로 가장 적합한 것은?

> A: Excuse me, could I interrupt?
> B: Of course
> A: I'd like to ask you about the "Ready Room".
> B: Sure. What exactly would you like to know?
> A: I am a presenter for this afternoon session C. I will be using the flip chart as well as the Powerpoint. There's quite a lot to cover through my talk which will last about 15 minutes.
> B: No problem. The Speaker's Room is arranged at Conference Room 312 for rehearsals. It is also staffed with technician.

(A) A: 통역사　　B: 연사

(B) A: 연사　　B: 진행요원

(C) A: 시청각 기자재 기술사　　B: 컨벤션 기획사

(D) A: 호텔직원　　B: 회의 참가자

[어휘] interrupt 방해하다 / last 지속하다

정답 I B

3. 국제회의 대표단은 여러 가지 덕목을 갖추어야 한다. 그 중에서 아래 글은 어떤 덕목의 중요성을 논하고 있는가?

> Try to see the problem through the eyes of other delegations. Even though your instructions are negative, you should be supportive of the general concerns expressed by others. The acknowledgement alone of a problem is often helpful and may even stimulate innovative solutions. Even if you feel superior, don't show it, and never underestimate your opposition. Do not let sex, religion, or nationality interfere with the substance of your negotiations.

(A) knowledge (B) patience

(C) attitude (D) sense of humor

[어휘] be supportive of 지지하는 / underestimate 과소평가하다 / substance 내용 정답 I C

Exercise

매년 12월에 열리는 노벨상 시상식은 스웨덴의 스톡홀름에서 개최됩니다. 노벨상 수상자들과 관계자들에게 보내는 초청장을 작성해볼까요?

The Nobel Prize Award Ceremony in the Stockholm Concert Hall

UNIT 13

For Convention(V)

Hotel
convention
English

호텔컨벤션영어

폐회사

국제회의의 개회사에 이어 이번에는 폐회사, Closing Address의 한 사례(2017 고령화 국제심포지엄)를 소개한다.

I. Opening Remarks

Honored guests and distinguished participants,
I'm OOO, Director General of the Survey and Management Bureau in Statistics Korea. It gives me great pleasure to make a few remarks at the closing ceremony of the Global Symposium on Ageing on behalf of the Commissioner of Statistics Korea OOO.

I would like to thank the respected Benoit Kalasa, Director of the Technical Division, UNFPA, honored members of parliaments, and the Asian Population and Development Association (APDA). Above all, I would like to thank all of you here, for your participation and for sharing your valuable insights and experience throughout the Symposium.

II. Result of Symposium

The main purpose of the Symposium was to review the fifteen years of progress made by each country in accordance with the Madrid International Plan of Action on Ageing (MIPAA) and to provoke a discussion on how each country can address the issues of population ageing.

During the past 2 days, experts from over 30 countries presented approximately 50 papers focusing on the three pillars of the MIPAA followed by meaningful and serious discussions. I am sure that the Symposium has successfully covered the progress of the MIPAA over the past fifteen years and reaped political and academic results on actions to be taken moving forward for population ageing.

The Global Symposium on Ageing was hosted by Statistics Korea and UNFPA as a part of a 5-year joint work project. Statistics Korea will continue to embrace the development of new theories and their applications. The United Nations (UN) is preparing the 2020 round of the World Population and Housing Censuses. The UNFPA is working on strengthening the statistical capacities of its member states.

In response to the demand from the international community, Statistics Korea will try its best to actively cooperate with the UNFPA and Intranational organizations to commit itself to the success of the world population and household census as well as the statistical development of developing countries. On this note, I would like to call upon all of you, experts from around the world, for your advice and collaboration.

III. Closing Remarks

Honored guests and distinguished participants,

I hope that each of you enjoy the beautiful autumn in Seoul and have a safe and pleasant journey back home. Lastly, I would like to extend my gratitude once again to members of the UNFPA, Statistics Korea, and the Asia Pacific Population Institute for their hard work. Thank you very much.

2017 고령화 국제심포지엄

폐 회 사

2017. 10.

조사관리국장

I. 인사말씀

안녕하십니까? 통계청 조사관리국장 OOO입니다.
통계청장을 대신하여 "2017 고령화 국제심포지엄"에서 폐회사를 하게 되어 영광입니다. 또한, Global Symposium on Ageing, Seoul 2017이 성공적으로 끝나게 되어 기쁩니다.

존경하는 OOO, 유엔인구기금(UNFPA) 본부 기술지원국장님, 아시아인구 및 개발협회(APDA) 회원으로 참석해 주신 각국의 국회의원 여러분께 특별히 감사드립니다. 그리고 끝까지 이 자리를 함께해 주시고, 지혜와 통찰과 경험을 공유해 주신 각 분야의 전문가 여러분들께도 감사인사 드립니다.

II. 심포지엄의 성과

이번 심포지엄은 지난 15년간 세계 각국에서 고령자의 건강과 웰빙을 위하여 노력한 결과를 평가하고, 앞으로 고령자 삶의 질을 높이기 위해 세계 각국의 실태와 고령화에 대처하는 방안을 찾는 중요한 심포지엄이었습니다. 어제, 오늘 양일간 마드리드 국제고령화선언(MIPAA)의 세 필라(Pillars)에 맞춰서 세계 30여 개국 전문가들이 약 50편의 논문을 발표하고 진지한 토론을 하였습니다.

이번 심포지엄을 통하여 마드리드 국제고령화선언(MIPAA) 15년간의 성과를 평가하고, 앞으로 고령화에 대한 적절한 대응을 위한 정책과 학문적 과실을 얻을 수 있었다고 확신합니다. 이번 고령화 국제심포지엄은 유엔인구기금(UNFPA)과 5개년 공동사업의 일환으로 개최되었습니다. 앞으로도 통계청은 인구분야 새로운 이론과 적용방법을 도입하고, 우리의 경험을 공유하는 노력을 계속할 것입니다. UN에서는 2020 라운드 세계인구센서스를 준비하고 있고, 유엔인구기금(UNFPA)에서는 각국의 통계작성 역량을 기르기 위하여 노력하고 있습니다.

한국 통계청에서는 이러한 국제적인 요구에 부응하여 앞으로 유엔인구기금(UNFPA)를 비롯하여 국제기구와의 협력으로 세계인구센서스의 성공은 물론 개발도상국의 인구통계 발전을 위하여 노력할 것입니다. 여기 계신 각계 전문가들의 조언과 협력을 이 자리를 빌려 부탁드립니다.

III. 맺음말

고령화 심포지엄을 빛내주신 전문가 여러분,
귀국하시기 전에 서울의 가을을 마음껏 즐기시고, 한 분 한 분 귀국하시는 길이 즐겁고 안전하시길 기원합니다. 끝으로 고령화 국제 심포지엄을 준비해 주신 유엔인구기금, 한국통계청과 아 · 태인구연구원 관계자들의 노고에 대해 다시 한 번 감사의 말씀을 드립니다. 감사합니다.

Writing Tips

1. 연사 초청편지

FIPP
SEOUL 2002

Date :

Dear ~ :

The International Federation of the Periodical Press(FIPP) and the Korean Magazine Association (KMA) are pleased to invite you to speak at the Asia-Pacific Magazine Media Regional Conference next April 16-18 in Seoul, Korea.

This is the first FIPP conference focusing exclusively on the opportunities and challenges of publishing in the rapidly developing magazine conference. It will be hosted by Korea and it will be the first FIPP Asian magazine conference to be held since the China Periodical Association joined FIPP last fall.

We would be very pleased to have you as one of the speakers in a session dedicated to the theme "~~~~~~~~." This is a very important question with challenges and opportunities to our industry in the "New World." Your insights would be a major contribution.

We expect a predominantly Asian audience of 300-500 delegates with strong support not only from the hosting Korean publishers but also from the Japan Magazine Publishers Association and the China Periodical Association. In addition, we expect delegates from Taiwan, Hong Kong, Australia and Southeast Asia as well.

So this will be an excellent opportunity for you to address and to network with a host of publishers from the Far East. You will also get a close look at Korea and its thriving Korean publishing industry together with social programmes designed to promote networking opportunities.

We sincerely believe this conference will be a unique and wonderful occasion, which you will enjoy along with us.

Sincerely yours,

Y.B. Min
Conference Chairman
Chairman, YBM Si-sa

Donald D. Kummerfeld
President
FIPP

[출처] FIPP(2002) 행사자료, www.fipp.com

Notes

focusing exclusively on 전적으로 ~에 초점을 둔
dedicated to ~에 바쳐진, 전적으로 ~를 다루는
delegates 대표자들
to address 말을 걸다, 발언하다, 연설하다

2. 연사 수락편지

SINGAPORE
INTERNATIONAL CONVENTION & EXHIBITION
C E N T R E
By Fax & Mail
31 March, 1998

Dr. ~~~
Graduate School of Studies on Convention Management

Hallym University, Korea

Dear Dr. ~~~
ACCEPTANCE OF INVITATION TO ICEM SYMPOSIUM & WORKSHOP - 23 & 24 JUNE '98

Thank you for your invitation to the ICEM Symposium & Workshop / We gladly accept your offer, and will be sending a speaker to the ICEM Symposium & Workshop in June. However, we can only furnish you with details of the speakers later.

Meanwhile, I would appreciate it if you could give me the full details of the symposium, such as deadline for materials, provision of translation services, AV set-up details, and electricity voltage requirements should we choose to bring our own equipment.

Let us also know if the Governor of Cheju Island, His Excellency Mr. Shin Boo Kum would be present at the symposium too.

Best regards, and looking forward to hearing from you.

Your sincerely,
SINGAPORE INTERNATIONAL
CONVENTION & EXHIBITION CENTRE

LAI CHEE KIONG
Director
Sales & Marketing

[출처] 컨벤션영어, 서승진·윤은주 공저

Notes

furnish A with B A에게 B를 제공하다
I would appreciate it if ~ ~해 준다면 고맙다
electricity watts requirements 전기와트 관련 필요조건들
His Excellency 대통령, 도지사 등 고위층 인사에게 예우로 이름 앞에 부르는 호칭

3. 연사 거절편지

UNLV

April 2, 1998

To: Dr. ~~~
Page 1 of 1
From: John Bowen

Dear Dr. ~~~
Thank you for your invitation to come to Korea and participate in the conference organized by your Institute of Convention and Event Management. it was quite an honor to receive the invitation.

Unfortunately, I am already committed during the period of your event. I am sorry that I will not be able to participate in the conference.

Thank you for thinking of me.

I am working on getting an equally qualified faculty member from UNLV that would be willing to come. If you think this person is qualified he could come in my place.

Best regards,
John Bowen

[출처] 컨벤션영어, 서승진 · 윤은주 공저

Notes

It was quite an honor to ~ ~하게 되어 매우 영광이다
I am working on ~ 나는 ~에 관해 연구 중이다
in my place 내 대신

Vocabulary

Write the word that best completes each sentence.

audience, invite, interrupt, announce, discussion

1. I am sorry to ______________ you.

2. We shall now turn to the ______________ for questions and comments.

3. Before proceeding to the vote, I would like to ______________ that France has joined the list of sponsors of the draft resolution.

4. The floor is now open for ______________.

5. I ______________ Mr. A to address the Assembly.

Global Countries and Culture

France

Paris: Regal and Intimate

성모마리아를 의미하는 노트르담(Notre-Dame) 성당 옆에 위치한 생쉴피스(Saint-Sulpice) 성당에는 유럽 최고의 파이프오르간이 있다. 그 연주자들의 목록 일번으로 요한 세바스찬 바흐의 이름이 올라있다.

Paris' original neighborhood, the Île de la Cité, is well worth exploring. While a church has stood on this island since ancient times, the iconic Gothic cathedral we see today — dedicated to "notre dame," or "Our Lady" — is only 700 years old.

You can brave the line for a look at its interior, and climb to the top of its bell tower. But the church I like to visit in Paris, especially on Sunday mornings, is St. Sulpice — to enjoy its magnificent pipe organ, arguably the greatest in Europe.

For organ lovers, a visit here is a pilgrimage. After Mass, enthusiasts from around the world scamper like 16th notes up the spiral stairs, into a world of 7,000 pipes.

Before electricity, it took three men, working out on these 18th-century Stairmasters, to fill the bellows, which powered the organ. The current organist,

Daniel Roth, carries on the tradition of welcoming guests into the loft to see the organ in action.

As his apprentices pull and push the many stops that engage the symphony of pipes, a commotion of music lovers crowd around a tower of keyboards and watch the master at work.

Saint-Sulpice has a rich history with a line of 12 world-class organists going back over 300 years. Like kings or presidents, the lineage is charted on the wall. And overseeing all this? Johann Sebastian Bach.

This sacred music continues to fill the spiritual sails of Saint-Sulpice as it has for centuries.

[출처] https://www.ricksteves.com

컨벤션기획사 영어시험문제

1. 다음은 국제회의 등록 서신 내용 중의 일부이다. (　　)에 들어갈 가장 적합한 표현은?

> Application for registration and reservations should be accompanied by a remittance of the fee. No registration and reservation will be confirmed (　　) these payments. Please send the cheque directly to Host Committee at the address.

(A) to the absence of　　(B) in the absence of

(C) by the absence of　　(D) for the absence of

[어휘] in the absence of = without

정답 I B

2. 다음 (　　)에 알맞은 표현은?

> As the symposium is fast approaching, we wish to urgently request that you send your presentation material (　　).

(A) whenever it is ready

(B) at your earliest convenience

(C) with donations to the scholarship fund

(D) after examination and review

[어휘] approach 다가오다 / request 부탁하다, 요청하다

정답 I B

3. 다음 문장에 대한 답신으로 가장 적합한 것은?

The Selection Committee will make an on-site visit to the final candidate cities, one of which is Seoul, prior to its final recommendation at the board of directors meeting. It is hoped that arrangements be made between April 3-10, 2017 for three members, two from san Francisco and one from Toronto. The committee would like to know if transportation and accommodation arrangements can be made during their visit.

(A) We will be pleased to have the Selection Committee members here in Seoul. However due to our busy schedule, April will not be suitable.

(B) We will make all the necessary arrangements and provide accommodation and transportation during your stay in Seoul.

(C) We meet our requirements in from April 3-10, 2017 for three members.

(D) Flight schedules from San Francisco and Toronto will be available upon request.

[어휘] upon request 요청에 의하여 / candidate city 입후보 도시

정답 I B

Exercise

국제회의에 참여한 인사들에게 보내는 만찬초대장을 작성해 볼까요?

Hotel
convention
English

호텔컨벤션영어

UNIT 14

For Convention(VI)

Hotel
convention
English

호텔컨벤션영어

축 사

국제회의의 개회사와 폐회사에 이어서 여기서는 Congratulatory Address의 한 사례(2017년 통계청 국제회의 시 OECD 대사의 축사)를 소개한다.

Congratulatory Remarks for KOSTAT Conference on “GDP plus Beyond”
OOO, Ambassador of Korea to the OECD

Commissioner OOO, Participants from academia and government, Ladies and Gentlemen,

It is my great honor to give the congratulatory remarks today. This conference is particularly meaningful at the current juncture when the world, including Korea, is voicing the need to revisit the economic-development paradigms. I am sure today's discussion on GDP and Beyond, which is about how to achieve a better life for all, will bring forth useful policy implications.

(GDP and its limitations)

As you are well aware, GDP has long been used as the key indicator to measure economic progress. Before GDP, there was no reliable macroeconomic indicator, so inevitably there were limitations in devising policy responses. Since the system of national accounts was developed in 1937, GDP has allowed us to assess the overall economic situation, and thereby construct appropriate policy prescriptions.

Nevertheless, GDP is not a sufficient statistic for our life. It has many limitations. For example, GDP does not differentiate between the creation of value-added with and without environmental pollution. Various aspects concerning the quality of life and income inequality are not properly captured by GDP.

(Measuring Beyond GDP)

Nevertheless, it would be unfair to blame GDP for not being a panacea for the multi-faceted aspects of life. We should rather devise alternative indicators. In this regard, recent discussions on Beyond GDP deserve our appreciation. For example, the Commission on the Measurement of Economic Performance and Societal Progress, established in 2008, advocated a shift in measurement emphasis from production to well-being. The G20 Summit in 2009 likewise affirmed that "G20 leaders should encourage work on measurement methods so as to better take into account the social and environmental dimensions."

(OECD's BLI and the UN's SDGs)

The OECD is one of the leading institutions in well-being discussions. Since 2004, the organization has held the World Forum on Statistics, Knowledge and Policy. Measuring the quality of life and social development has been at the heart of the Forum discussions. Such activities have contributed to the OECD's mission of promoting "Better Policies for Better Lives."

Since 2011, the OECD has published the Better Life Index (BLI). Consisting of 24 indicators from 11 dimensions, such as income, jobs, housing, health, and environment, the BLI provides a measure of the quality of life. The Index helps us understand the well-being status of a country and identify areas where improvement is needed.

Today's theme of GDP and Beyond is also related to the UN's Sustainable Development Goals (SDGs). Adopted in 2015, the SDGs present a set of 17 goals and 169 targets to ensure the prosperity of humankind. Each country is preparing to achieve the goals through assessing its current situation, designing implementation strategies, and establishing its policy framework.

These Beyond-GDP indicators have particular implications for Korea. In the case of the BLI, Korea ranks highly in the economic dimensions, but its social and environmental performance has been poor. Addressing this dichotomy between economic and social progress is clearly overdue.

The SDG framework will be particularly useful for Korea in assessing its structural problems and revisiting the relevance of the existing development strategies. In this context, I would like to express my appreciation for the efforts of Statistics Korea in establishing the SDG monitoring framework.

Despite the progress in measuring GDP and Beyond-GDP, many areas require further research. Beyond-GDP indicators provide a useful check-up list of our society's health, but their reliability and comparability should be improved. We also need to better understand trade-offs and synergies among policy goals. Today's discussions will shed light on improving the related policy framework.

(Closing Remarks)

Ladies and gentlemen,

The development of statistics has reflected the challenges of each era. In the 17th century, European governments compiled national wealth statistics in order to expand their revenues forwards. In the 20th century, GDP gained prominence, reflecting the longing for a material progress. Now, we are facing the challenges of achieving inclusive and sustainable growth and enhancing th equality of life. There should be constant efforts to address these contemporary demands by better measuring economic and social development.

I look forward to our constructive and fruitful discussions today.
Thank you.

통계청 국제컨퍼런스 축사

OECD 대사 OOO

OOO 통계청장님 그리고 이 자리에 참석하신 학계, 정부 및 관계 전문가 여러분! 오늘 행사에서 축사를 하게 된 것을 매우 기쁘게 생각합니다. 오늘 컨퍼런스는 우리나라를 비롯한 국내 · 외에서 발전 패러다임에 대한 재검토 요구가 커지고 있는 현 시점에서 특별한 의미가 있다고 생각합니다. 오늘 컨퍼런스는 대다수 국민의 삶의 질을 어떻게 향상시킬 것인지에 대해 유용한 정책적 시사점을 제공할 것으로 기대합니다.

(GDP 유용성과 한계)

주지하시다시피, GDP는 일국의 경제발전을 측정하는 대표 지표로 활용되어 왔습니다. GDP 이전에는 신뢰할 만한 경제지표가 없어 정책대응에 한계가 있었습니다. 국민계정(National Accounts) 체계가 개발된 후 경제상황 판단과 올바른 정책대응이 가능해졌습니다.

그러나 GDP는 삶의 질에 관한 충분한 정보를 제공하지 못한다는 한계도 함께 지적되어 왔습니다. 예를 들어, 환경오염을 초래하는 부가가치와 그렇지 않은 부가가치는 다르게 측정될 필요성이 있습니다. 또한, GDP가 삶의 질과 소득불평등 등 다양한 측면을 제대로 반영하지 못한다는 문제점도 제기되고 있습니다.

(Beyond GDP 측정)

GDP가 삶의 다양한 측면을 반영하지 못한다는 이유만으로 GDP의 유용성을 낮게 평가하는 것은 옳지 않다고 생각합니다. 그보다는 삶의 다양한 측면을 측정할 수 있는 별도 지표를 개발하는 방안을 모색해야 합니다. 이러한 측면에서, Beyond GDP에 대한 그간의 논의는 환영할만합니다. 2008년 발족한 경제 및 사회발전 측정위원회는 경제사회 발전을 측정하는데 있어 기존 생산 중심에서 웰빙 중심으로의 전환 필요성을 강조하였습니다. 2009년 G20 정상회의에서는 사회 및 환경 측면을 감안하여 경제사회 발전을 다면적으로 측정하는 것이 필요하다는 데 합의한 바 있습니다.

(OECD의 BLI 및 UN 지속가능개발목표)

웰빙 관련 연구와 정책을 선도하는 기관 중 하나가 OECD입니다. OECD는 2004년부터 세계포럼(World Forum on Statistics, Knowledge and Policy)을 개최하며 삶의 질과 사회발전 측정에 관한 연구를 진행하였습니다. 이러한 행보는 '보다 나은 삶을 위한 보다 나은 정책(Better Policies for Better Lives)'이라는 OECD 목표에도 부합됩니다.

OECD는 2011년부터 웰빙 수준을 측정하는 Better Life Index를 발표하고 있습니다. 이 지표는 주거, 소득, 직업, 환경, 건강 등 11개 영역의 24개 지표로 구성되어 있습니다. 이를 통해 각국의 웰빙 수준과 개선이 필요한 분야를 가늠할 수 있게 되었습니다.

오늘 컨퍼런스 주제는 UN 지속가능발전목표(Sustainable Development Goals)와도 큰 연관성이 있습니다. 2015년 채택된 SDG는 인류가 공통으로 갖추어야 할 삶의 기준을 17개 목표, 169개 타깃으로 제시한 것입니다. 현재 각국은 SDG 초기상황을 평가하고 목표달성 전략과 추진체계를 정비하는 등 이행을 위해 노력하고 있습니다.

이러한 Beyond GDP 지표가 갖는 의미와 유용성은 우리나라에 특히 크다고 생각합니다. Better Life Index에서 우리나라는 경제 관련지표의 경우 상위권에 랭크돼 있으나, 사회·환경지표는 하위권에 머물러 있어 이에 대한 대응이 시급한 상황입니다.

SDG는 우리나라의 구조적 문제를 진단하고, 발전전략을 재검토하는 계기로서 의미가 있다고 생각합니다. 이러한 맥락에서, 현재 통계청의 SDG 모니터링 프레임워크 구축을 위한 노력을 높게 평가하는 바입니다.

GDP 및 Beyond GDP 지표 개발과 관련하여 그간 가시적인 성과가 있었으나, 심층적인 연구가 필요한 분야 또한 많이 있습니다. Beyond GDP 지표가 우리 사회의 건강상태를 점검하는데 유용한 도구이지만, 동 지표들의 비교가능성과 신뢰성을 높일 필요가 있습니다. 정책목표의 상충성과 시너지에 대해서도 깊이 있는 연구가 필요합니다. 오늘 컨퍼런스에서의 논의가 이에 기여할 수 있기를 바랍니다.

(맺음말)

친애하는 참석자 및 전문가 여러분,

통계의 개발과 발전에는 당시의 시대적 요구가 반영돼 있다고 생각합니다. 17세기 유럽에서는 전시 재정확충을 위해 국부통계를 작성하였으며, 20세기 물질적인 발전이 필요했던 시기에는 GDP 통계가 중시되었습니다. 이제 우리는 지속가능한 성장과 삶의 질 향상이라는 시대적 요구에 직면하고 있습니다. 이러한 도전과제에 효과적으로 대응하기 위해 경제 및 사회 지표의 개선을 위한 꾸준한 노력이 필요한 시점이라고 생각합니다.

오늘 회의에서 다양하고 건설적인 논의가 있기를 기원합니다.

감사합니다.

Writing Tips

1. 참가자에게 보내는 감사편지

April 22, 2002

Dear

We would like to thank you personally as well as on behalf of FIPP and the Korea Magazine Association for your presence at the FIPP Asia-Pacific Magazine Media Regional Conference 2002 held from the 16th to the 18th of April in Seoul, Korea.

The FIPP Seoul Conference 2002 which ran under the theme "Magazine Media Welcome the Digital Age" was a great success thanks to almost 600 magazine leaders of the world who did not leave the venue until the last moment of the Conference, let alone to many precious speeches and papers presented by prominent speakers.

Without your active participation and enthusiastic support, we strongly believe, this gathering could not have been a fruitful, pleasurable and rewarding one. Let us extend our deepest appreciation once again for your contribution and cooperation to make this conference a never-to-be-forgotten event.

Y.B. Min
Conference Chairman
Chairman, YBM Si-sa

Donald D. Kummerfeld
President
FIPP

[출처] FIPP(2002) 행사자료

Notes

personally as well as on behalf of~ ~를 대신해서뿐 아니라 개인적으로도
thanks to ~덕분에
venue 개최장소
let alone ~는 말할 것도 없이
gathering 모임
never-to-be-forgotten 잊을 수 없는

2. 감사편지

Dear IEA 2003 Booth visitors,

Thank you for visiting our IEA 2003 booth in the IEA / HFES 2000 San Diego Congress. We, the IEA 2003 Organizing Committee and Secretariat staff, are doing our best to make the IEA 2003 Seoul Congress a great success. As you watched the film introducing the venue and KOREA in the closing ceremony of IEA 2000, the ASEM Convention Center is the newest and best convention facility in Asia. You can enjoy a dynamic and variable experience during your stay in Seoul along with your participation at the Congress. We promise that we will provide you a well-organized program with a variety of subjects. If you have any questions, don't hesitate to contact us.

We hope see all of you in the IEA 2003 Seoul Congress

IEA 2003 Secretariat
Kang Nam P.O. Box 467 Seoul, KOREA 135-646
Tel: +82-2-3446-2451
Fax: +82-2-3446-2465

[출처] IEA(2003) 행사자료, www.iea.org

Notes

the closing ceremony 폐회식
along with ~와 함께

Vocabulary

Write the word that best completes each sentence.

conclude, appreciation, quoting, grateful, journey

1. I would like to express our acknowledgements and ______________ to our Secretary General and his staff.

2. I am also ______________ to the interpreters for the outstanding work they have performed during these two weeks.

3. It's time to ______________ the session.

4. I wish you a pleasant ______________ home and we look forward to meeting all of you again in Seoul next year.

5. I would like to come to a close by ______________ Mr. A, the famous philosopher who said....

Global Countries and Culture

France

Normandy

노르망디지방의 최고의 절경은 단연코 '몽생미쉘'(Mont Saint-Michel)이다. 마법의 건축물로 불려지는, 바다 한 가운데 바위섬 꼭대기에 세워진 수도원은, 매년 방문객이 늘고 있고, 이젠 행글라이더로 주위를 둘러볼 수 있는 하늘관광 프로그램이 인기를 끌고 있다.

Our next stop — an hour's drive away — is Mont St-Michel. For over a thousand years, the silhouette of this island abbey has sent pilgrim's weary spirits soaring. Today it does the same for tourists. Mont St-Michel, [mon san mee-shell] which through the ages has been among the top pilgrimage sites in Christendom, floats like a mirage on the horizon.

The vast Bay of Mont St-Michel, which turns into a mudflat at low tide, has long played a key role here. Since the sixth century, hermit monks came here in search of solitude.

The word "hermit" comes from an ancient Greek word meaning "desert." The closest thing to a desert in this part of Europe was the sea. Imagine the "desert" this bay provided as the first monk climbed that rock to get nearer to God.

The rock, capped by an abbey, was even more isolated by its mythic tides.

Pilgrims crossed the mudflat quickly and carefully knowing that the sea swept in "at the speed of a galloping horse."

In the late 1800s, a road was built, connecting the island to the mainland and letting pilgrims come and go without hip boots.

The town of Mont St-Michel — with only 30 residents — entertains over 2 million tourists a year. Its main street — lined with shops and hotels leading up to the abbey — is grotesquely commercial. It's some consolation to remember that, even back in the Middle Ages, this was a retail gauntlet, with stalls selling souvenir medallions, candles, and fast food like omelets.

An island specialty is quick, tasty, and extremely fluffy omelets. They were popular for eat-and-run pilgrims who needed to beat the tide and they remain a hit with visitors today. Enjoy the show as cooks make sure the traditional beat goes on.

[출처] https://www.ricksteves.com

컨벤션기획사 영어시험문제

1. ( )에 들어갈 가장 적합한 내용은?

> Mr. Chairman, I'd like to suggest at this time that a small committee be appointed to work out a compromise proposal. We have already spent two days discussing the question. It seems to be me that we are agreed on what the end result should be, but cannot agree on the means to achieve that end. I have no doubt that, from the many suggestions that have been offered during our discussions, some compromise can be worked out. I would therefore like to propose to this conference that ( ).

(A) I am of the opinion that the proposal which has just been made is quite to the point.

(B) I am afraid I cannot agree with the opinion of the delegates

(C) I'd like to say a few words in connection with the opinion expressed by the delegates.

(D) the chairman appoint a committee of two delegates from each side to draft a compromise proposal.

[어휘] compromise 화해, 타협

정답 I D

2. 다음의 내용에서 연사에게 제공되는 사항은?

> As an invited speaker, you will receive business class airfare and hotel accommodations, per diem, in addition to an honorarium of USD 2,000. We well make all of the necessary miscellaneous arrangements for your trip.

(A) 강연료, 항공, 호텔, 일비

(B) 강연료, 항공, 숙식

(C) 숙식, 항공, 공항영접, 일비

(D) 체재비, 호텔, 항공, 그 외 발생 가능한 사항

[어휘] per diem 일일경비

정답 I A

3. 다음 글에 내포된 정보 내용과 일치하는 것은?

At present, the largest convention center in the U.S. is Chicago's McCormick Place, which offers 2.2 million square feet of exhibit space... and 371,365 square feet of meeting space. Nashville's Opryland Hotel, with nearly 300,00 square feet of exhibit space, is the largest hotel facility and will continue to be until the opening of Opryland Hotels in Kissimmee, Florida, in 2004 and Grapevine, Texas, in 2005. Each will offer 400,000 square feet of exhibit space.

(A) McCormick Place 컨벤션센터의 회의장 면적은 전시장 면적보다 넓다.

(B) 현재 미국 내의 호텔 중 가장 넓은 전시장을 갖춘 것은 Nashville에 있으며, 이 호텔은 2005년까지 미국에서 호텔로서는 가장 넓은 전시장을 갖춘 것으로 남을 것이다.

(C) Kissimmee에 지을 Opryland Hotel의 전시장 면적과 Grapevine에 지을 Opryland Hotel의 전시장 면적을 합치면 40만 평방피트이다.

(D) Kissimmee에 지을 Opryland Hotel의 전시장 면적과 Grapevine에 지을 Opryland Hotel의 전시장 면적은 서로 똑같다.

[어휘] exhibit space 전시공간, 전시장 면적

정답 I D

Exercise

국제회의에 참여했던 연사에게 보내는 감사편지를 작성해 볼까요? 아래 문제는 컨벤션 기획사 2급 제6회 모의고사에 제출되었던 문제입니다.

Q. FIPP 서울대회 조직위원장인 홍길동과 FIPP president인 K.L. Miller가 Dentsu 회사의 Media Services / Magazine Division의 Director이고, 연사였던 Toshiharu Kanesaka 씨에게 보내는 감사편지를 영어로 작성하시오.

[출처] www.yahoo.com(The World meets in Bonn, Bonn International)

Hotel
convention
English

호텔컨벤션영어